NEW EDITION

D1646081

Elementary
Vocabulary

B J THOMAS

WITHDRAWN FROM
BROMLEY LIBRARIES

Longman

BROMLEY LIBRARIES

3 0128 02513 9497

Pearson Education Limited
Edinburgh Gate
Harlow, Essex CM20 2JE, England
and associated companies throughout the world.

www.longman.com

© B J Thomas 1990

First published by Edward Arnold,
a division of Hodder and Stoughton Ltd

Eleventh impression 2006

Second and subsequent editions first published by Thomas Nelson and Sons Ltd 1990

This (revised) edition published by Addison Wesley Longman Limited 1996

ISBN-13: 978-0-17-557128-4
ISBN-10: 0-17-557128-7

All rights reserved. No part of this publication may be reproduced, stored in a retrieval system, or transmitted in any form or by any means, electronic, mechanical, photocopying, recording or otherwise, without the prior written permission of the Publishers.

Printed in Malaysia, PA

Illustrated by Gillian Martin, Dave Remnant

BROMLEY PUBLIC LIBRARIES	
02513949	
Bertrams	15.12.06
428.24	£9.90
BECAPB	

Contents

Introduction

Elementary Vocabulary is for students who are doing a beginner's course in English and wish to check and expand their basic vocabulary. Students at intermediate level will also find it useful for checking and testing themselves. The book presents essential words from a variety of common, everyday topic areas, vocabulary which all learners will need to know at an early stage of their studies. The varied and enjoyable exercises include gap-filling, matching and word-building.

To the student

If you are studying without a teacher, do not simply go through the book 'filling in the blanks'. When you learn new words, practise them and note the spelling before you do other exercises. It is not enough simply to *understand* new words: if you want the words to become part of your active vocabulary, you must *use* them in conversation, composition or letters.

To the teacher

Elementary Vocabulary is divided into eight sections, each presenting words on a different basis of selection and in a variety of exercises in which words are contextualised. *Dictionary Practice* is provided by the first section. The next two sections, *Topics* and *How to ...*, contain words and phrases in basic topic areas such as *Shopping* and *How to use a Cassette Player*, and include items useful for students writing about or discussing a particular topic. The fourth section, *Related Word Groups*, contains sets of essential adjectives, verbs and nouns which students should know before proceeding to the intermediate level. The fifth section, *Word Building*, encourages students to be aware of how words are formed and should help them to deduce the meanings of unknown words by recognising common patterns in word formation. The sixth section, *Idioms*, is an introduction to the everyday idiomatic usage of common vocabulary. The seventh section, *Miscellaneous*, is a reference section giving invaluable, practical information on the most common abbreviations and rules of pronunciation and spelling. *Word Games* provides spelling and vocabulary practice through a variety of exercises.

Throughout the book there are 'information boxes' containing interesting information about words and their usage.

Elementary Vocabulary can be used in a variety of ways. Exercises will probably be most effective if students do them only after the subject matter has been introduced and explained. The book should not be used to give students a series of mechanical tests. Exercises can be done as pair or group activities in class, followed by discussion or other creative tasks in which the students are required to use the words they have learnt. Simpler exercises can be done as homework, after suitable class preparation or with the aid of the key or a dictionary.

Note: a companion volume, *Intermediate Vocabulary*, also contains a number of exercises suitable for elementary learners and these exercises will supplement the material in this book.

Dictionary Practice

Use a good dictionary to do the following exercises. If you like, you can try to do them without help first, but check your answers in a dictionary afterwards.

Finding words

Put the following words into alphabetical order.

book	boy	bath	both	biscuit
break	bicycle	burn	bank	blood

Finding pronunciation

1   In which of the following words is the -o pronounced /ɒ/ as in 'hot' and in which is it pronounced /ʌ/ as in 'come'?

wrong	donkey	among	across	son
company	monkey	love	gone	bomb
nothing	shop	mother	done	Monday

2   In which of the following words is the -h **not** pronounced?

home	house	hour	exhausted	hair
honest	honour	high	hope	exhibition

3   In each of the following four-word groups underline the **two** words with **exactly the same pronunciation**.
e.g. <u>peace</u>   peas   pace   <u>piece</u> (both words are pronounced /piːs/)

sew	so	sir	saw		toe	too	two	tar
still	steel	style	steal		mail	male	mile	mill
fear	fur	fair	fare		wait	white	wheat	weight
her	here	hear	hair		bar	bear	bare	beer

Finding stress

Mark the stressed syllable in the words below.
e.g. 'beautiful   under'stand   'finish

begin	offer	photograph	photographic	breakfast
open	prefer	photographer	important	appointment

Finding spelling

1   What is the correct spelling of the -ing forms ('playing', 'sitting') of the following verbs?

hope	lie	picnic	write	put
stop	hit	travel	begin	die

2 Finish the spelling of the words below with the correct endings from those above each group.

-s -es (noun plurals)

radio_	hero_	studio_	piano_	cargo_
potato_	kilo_	echo_ .	photo_	video_

-er -or -ar

li_	beginn_	begg_	prison_	translat_
own_	bachel_	auth_	burgl_	inspect_

3 Correct the spelling mistakes in the following words.

hollyday	sistem	seperate	proffeser	accomodation
allways	adress	greatful	imediately	responsable

Finding meaning

1 Divide the following word groups into groups of equal number below the correct headings above each group.

parts of a book   parts of the body

index	thigh	contents	ankle	chapter
chest	thumb	cover	page	wrist

clothing parts   human sounds   things in our pockets

wallet	belt	ticket	yawn	cuff
sniff	comb	lining	zip	purse
lapel	cough	key	sneeze	hiccup

2 Each of the following words can be used as a noun and also, with a completely different meaning, as a verb. Give a simple example of each.
e.g. **book** I read a book. I booked a ticket for the theatre.

suit   match   box   sink   iron

Finding different word parts

1 Put the past tense of the verbs into the sentences.
(a) She _____ the class history. *(teach)*
(b) He _____ in the war. *(fight)*
(c) They _____ stones at the dog. *(throw)*
(d) The river _____ last night. *(freeze)*
(e) He _____ the beer quickly *(drink)*
(f) She _____ to stay at home. *(prefer)*

2 For each phrase below give a word beginning with 'night' which has the same meaning, e.g. garment worn by a woman in bed (Answer: nightdress)

terrible, frightening dream
hours of darkness
time of day when it gets dark
last drink, usually alcoholic, before going to bed

Topics

The Family

1   Look at the picture and then put the correct words in the sentences.

son   aunt   niece   cousins   husband   daughter   children
wife   uncle   sister   nephew   parents   brother

(a)   Bill is Vera's _____, so of course she's Bill's _____.
(b)   Bill and Vera have two _____, Ray and Kate.
(c)   Ray and Amy have a _____, Jill, and a _____, Joe.
(d)   Joe is Jill's _____ and Jill is Joe's _____.
(e)   Di and Don's _____ are Kate and Bob.
(f)   Jill and Joe are Di and Don's _____.
(g)   Bob is Jill and Joe's _____. Kate is their _____.
(h)   Jill is the _____ of Kate and Bob. Joe is their _____.

2   Instructions as above.

grandson   grandparents   granddaughter   son-in-law
father-in-law   grandchildren   grandmother   sister-in-law
brother-in-law   grandfather   mother-in-law   daughter-in-law

(a)   Bill and Vera have four _____, Joe, Jill, Di and Don.
(b)   Bill and Vera are the _____ of Joe, Jill, Di and Don.
(c)   Don is Bill's _____. Bill is Don's _____.
(d)   Vera is Di's _____. Di is Vera's _____.
(e)   Amy isn't the daughter of Bill and Vera. She's their _____.
(f)   Bill is Amy's _____ and Vera is her _____.
(g)   Kate isn't Amy's real sister. She's her _____.
(h)   Bob is Ray's _____ and he's the _____ of Bill and Vera.

3   Give the following relationships.
e.g. Ray and Di = uncle and niece

(a)   Di and Don   (e)   Kate and Jill   (i)   Bob and Ray
(b)   Bob and Di   (f)   Ray and Don   (j)   Vera and Don
(c)   Vera and Ray   (g)   Bill and Bob   (k)   Bill and Jill
(d)   Don and Joe   (h)   Bob and Kate   (l)   Vera and Amy

3

Transport

1 Match each of the following words with the correct letter in the picture below.

(aero)plane	car	ship	motor-bike (motor-cycle)
lorry	bus	train	bike (bicycle)
helicopter	van	boat	underground train

2 Put the correct verbs from the following list in the passage below. If necessary, add -s or -es.

reach   wait   get(2)   take(2)   pay   go   arrive

I sometimes (a) _____ to school on foot, but usually I (b) _____ a bus because it's quicker by bus. I (c) _____ for the bus at the bus-stop. When it (d) _____ at the stop, I (e) _____ on and (f) _____ my fare. When the bus (g) _____ the school, I (h) _____ off. The journey (i) _____ about half an hour.

3 Use the correct word from the following list, *or nothing,* in the sentences.

off   on   at   for   by   to

(a) Ann went _____ school _____ bus today, not _____ foot.
(b) She waited _____ the bus _____ the bus-stop.
(c) When the bus arrived _____ the bus-stop, she got _____.
(d) Finally the bus reached _____ the school bus-stop and Ann got _____.

4 Describe how you (a) go to school or work, (b) made a long journey.

Parts of the Body

1   Match each word in the following list with the correct letter in the pictures below.

bottom	knee	chest	neck	leg	sole	foot (pl: feet)
tongue	arm	toes	ear	eye	back	tooth (pl: teeth)
shoulder	hair	waist	head	lips	mouth	
fingers	hand	thumb	heel	nose	elbow	

2   Complete the following sentences with the correct words from Exercise 1.

(a)   We pick things up with our _____.

(b)   I lick an ice-cream with my _____.

(c)   To eat something, I put it in my _____.

(d)   We comb and brush our _____.

(e)   He had a cold and blew his _____.

(f)   I brush my _____ regularly, especially after eating.

Clothes

1   Match each word in the following list with the correct letter in the pictures below.

blouse	casual jacket	cap	jeans	suit	belt
jacket	underwear	tie	shoes	dress	socks
sweater	tee-shirt	hat	boots	shorts	skirt
overcoat	trousers	shirt			

2   Put the correct words from the following list in the sentences below.

on   in   with

(a)   He's dressed _____ a dark suit.
(b)   She's got a yellow dress _____.
(c)   Who's the man _____ the red tie?
(d)   Maria's the girl _____ the white blouse and black skirt.
(e)   It was very cold. He had an overcoat _____.
(f)   I remember her. She was the one _____ green shoes.

3   Describe how you or a friend are dressed using the phrases in Exercise 2 (or simply 'He's wearing _____') and adjectives like old, new, smart, casual, clean, dirty, red, blue etc.

Bathroom and Bedroom

1   Match each word in the following list with the correct letter in the picture below.

toilet	bed	blanket	hanger	dressing-gown	tiles
stool	bath	nightdress	pillow	chest of drawers	
mirror	sheets	wardrobe	pyjamas	wash-basin	

2   Complete the following sentences with the correct words from Exercise 1.
(a)   We hang trousers, jackets and dresses in the _____.
(b)   We keep shirts and underwear in the _____.
(c)   I sleep with my head on the _____.
(d)   I wash my hands in the _____.
(e)   We sleep between the _____ under a warm _____.
(f)   I take my _____ off before I go to bed.

3   Put the correct words from the following list in the sentences below.

on   in   to

(a)   I put an extra blanket _____ my bed.
(b)   I hang my clothes _____ hangers _____ the wardrobe.
(c)   I go _____ bed at midnight.
(d)   I put my head _____ the pillow.
(e)   I sat _____ the stool.
(f)   I keep underwear _____ the chest of drawers.

4   Cover the words in Exercise 1 and name the things in the picture.

Living room

1 Match each word in the following list with the correct letter in the picture below.

switch	sofa	rug	armchair	cushion	television
lamp	light	mat	radio	bookcase	waste-paper bin
ceiling	floor	fan	carpet		

2 Complete the following sentences with the correct words from Exercise 1.
(a) I watch _____ while I am sitting on the _____ or in an _____.
(b) I sometimes listen to the _____.
(c) If it's too hot, I put on the _____.
(d) I keep my books in a _____.
(e) I don't keep old letters. I put them in the _____.
(f) I put a _____ on the sofa to make it more comfortable.

3 Put the correct words from the following list in the sentences below.

in   on   to

(a) Put _____ the fan.
(b) The books are _____ the bookcase.
(c) He was listening _____ the radio.
(d) She sat _____ an armchair.
(e) They were sitting _____ the sofa.
(f) Put it _____ the waste-paper bin.

4 Cover the words in Exercise 1 and name the things in the picture.

In the Street

1   Match each word in the following list with the correct letter in the picture below.

kerb	car park	queue	litter-bin
signs	post-box	poster	parking warden
road	lamp-post	pavement	traffic-lights
bus-stop	gutter	crossroads	railings
crossing	parking meter	pedestrians (people on foot)	

2   Complete the following sentences with the correct words from Exercise 1.
(a)   We stand in a _____ to wait for a bus at a _____.
(b)   The cars wait until the _____ turn to green.
(c)   You can cross the road at a _____.
(d)   Big advertisements are called _____s.
(e)   We should put waste paper in a _____.
(f)   A _____ has to make sure that motorists use _____s correctly.

3   Put the correct words from the following list in the sentences below.

on   at   in   to

(a)   You can leave your car _____ a car park or _____ a parking meter.
(b)   They stood _____ a queue _____ the bus-stop.
(c)   Put that _____ a litter-bin.
(d)   The traffic-lights have turned _____ red.
(e)   The pedestrian was just standing _____ the pavement.

4   Cover the words in Exercise 1 and name the things in the picture.

The Seaside

1   Match each word in the following list with the correct letter in the picture below.

rocks	sand	cliff	sea	motor-boat
wave	canoe	tent	horizon	sailing boat
kayak	stones	hotel	bungalow	swimming-costume
pier	towel	beach	sunshade	rowing boat

2   Cover the words in Exercise 1 and name the things in the picture. Use the following phrases.

on the left

in the background
in the middle
in the foreground

on the right

One Word or Two?

1 **Cannot** and **another** must normally each be written as one word only.

2 Some expressions are written as one word or two depending on their meaning.

He swims **every day**. (adverb phrase, like **every week**, **every month** etc.)
It's an **everyday** word. (adjective, meaning **ordinary**, **not special**)

She **may be** ill. (verb phrase, meaning **is possibly**, **might be**)
Maybe she's ill. (adverb, meaning **perhaps**, **possibly**)

The Country

1   Match each word in the following list with the correct letter in the picture below.

bridge	valley	hill	sheep and lamb	tractor
farm	stream	forest	cow and calf	chicken and chick
waterfall	wood	barn	horse and foal	
field	pond	spade	duck and duckling	

2   Cover the words in Exercise 1 and name the things in the picture.

The House

1   Match each word in the following list with the correct letter in the picture below.

curtain	blind	roof	shutter
aerial	fence	path	door
chimney	stairs	gate	garage
garden	floor	wall	satellite dish

2   Cover the words in Exercise 1 and name the things in the picture.

Common, Proper and Abstract Nouns

Common nouns:	ordinary nouns, e.g. cat, window, man, food
Proper nouns:	names of particular people, places, events, times etc.: Bob Smith, Russia, River Amazon, Olympic Games, Christmas, Wednesday, April
Abstract nouns:	ideas and feelings we cannot see or touch e.g. happiness, democracy, fear, courage

The Weather

1 Match each of the following words with the correct picture.

forecast   cloud   fog   mist   sun   snow   wind   rain

2 Put each of the following adjectives in the correct space in the passage below.

wet	hot	freezing	cold	clear
dry	mild	changeable	warm	cloudy

I always watch the weather forecast on television to see what tomorrow's weather will be like. In England the weather changes very often. It's very (a) _____. Sometimes it rains for a day or two, but after the (b) _____ weather, often with noisy thunderstorms, it is sometimes (c) _____ for a long time, with no rain at all. On some days the sun shines and the sky is (d) _____, but on other days it is so (e) _____ you can't see the sun. The summers aren't usually very (f) _____ but the temperature usually reaches 25°, so it's quite (g) _____. In winter it is sometimes quite (h) _____ and pleasant but sometimes it's very (i) _____ or even (j) _____. The climate isn't very good for holidays but it makes the countryside green.

3 Finish each sentence on the left below with the correct verb on the right.

(a) We get wet when it	(1) shines.
(b) When it's very cold, everything	(2) rains.
(c) Children enjoy playing games when it	(3) blows.
(d) It's cold in England when a north wind	(4) freezes.
(e) It's warm and pleasant when the sun	(5) pours.
(f) When it rains very heavily, it	(6) snows.

4 What's the weather like in your country?

Passive and Active Vocabulary

Your **passive vocabulary**: the words and phrases you recognise, know and understand even if you cannot use them all with confidence.

Your **active vocabulary**: the words and phrases you not only understand but can use confidently yourself.

Which is bigger, your active or your passive vocabulary?

You can increase your passive vocabulary by reading, listening and using books like this. You can increase your active vocabulary by **using** these words in conversation and writing.

Going Shopping

1 Match each of the following words with the correct item in the picture.

shelves   customers   check-out   cashier   trolley
queue   assistant   till   manager   basket

2 Put each of the following words or phrases in the correct space in the passage below.

pay   push   find   spend   take
buy   sell   need   complain   look for

I love shopping. I love looking round the shops and seeing all the things and all the people. My friends say I like to (a) _____ money. It's probably true. There's a very good supermarket near me. They have everything you (b) _____ for your house. If you want a tin of sardines, a tube of toothpaste, a box of chocolates, a carton of milk, a packet of biscuits, a bottle of beer or a jar of jam, you can (c) _____ it at the supermarket. They (d) _____ everything. If you want a lot of things, you can use a trolley and (e) _____ it in front of you. If you don't want much, you can use a small basket. Then (f) _____ the things you want. If you can't (g) _____ them on the shelves, ask an assistant for help. When you see what you want, you just (h) _____ it from the shelves and put it in the trolley. When you have everything, you must stand in the queue at the check-out to (i) _____. Give your money to the cashier. He or she will put it in the till and give you your change. If there is anything wrong, if the service isn't good, customers can (j) _____ to the manager. Our supermarket is super.

3   Put the correct word or phrase from the following list in each space.

from   round   in front of   for   on   at   in   to

(a) Before I buy, I look _____ the shop.
(b) I must buy some things _____ my house.
(c) You can buy almost everything _____ the supermarket.
(d) I pushed the trolley _____ me.
(e) There's some nice fruit _____ that shelf.
(f) I asked an assistant _____ some help.
(g) I took some biscuits _____ the shelf.
(h) I put the bottles _____ my trolley.
(i) I had to wait _____ a queue.
(j) I gave the correct money _____ the cashier.

4   Match each of the following words with the correct picture.

jar   carton   tin   bottle   tube   box   packet

In which of the above containers do we usually buy the following things?
Sometimes more than one answer is possible.
E.g. soup: tin or packet

(h) wine
(i) matches
(j) glue
(k) fruit juice
(l) face cream
(m) marmalade

(n) fruit salad
(o) honey
(p) sugar
(q) cigarettes
(r) paint
(s) rice

5   On the left below are phrases we often use in shops. Match each one to the assistant's correct reply on the right.

(a) Can I try this jacket on?   (1) Of course, if you have some kind of bank card.
(b) Does this jacket suit me?   (2) I'm afraid we don't give refunds.
(c) Does this jacket fit me?   (3) Certainly. There's a changing room over there.
(d) Can I pay by cheque?   (4) It's a little too long. Try a smaller size.
(e) I'm afraid I only have a £10 note. (5) If you have a receipt.
(f) Can I exchange this?   (6) That's all right. I can change it.
(g) Can I have my money back?   (7) Yes, it's just the right colour and style for you.

Work

1 Match each word or phrase on the left below with the correct phrase on the right.

(a) **wages**   (1) certificates and exams passed
(b) **skills**   (2) a talk with a company about a possible job
(c) **experience**   (3) the times when you work
(d) **qualifications**   (4) points in your character (politeness, honesty etc.)
(e) **interview**   (5) abilities, things you can do (type, drive etc.)
(f) **hours**   (6) work of the same type you have done before
(g) **personal qualities** (7) money you get, usually hourly or weekly ('salary' is usually monthly or annually)

2 Put each of the words on the left in Exercise 1 above in the correct space in the following conversation.

Valerie: Hello, I'm Valerie Woods. I've come for an (a) _____ for a job as a secretary.

Mr Watts: Oh yes, Miss Woods. Please take a seat. Well, have you done office work before? Have you any (b) _____?

Valerie: Well, I'm afraid I haven't. I've just left college. But I have some (c) _____. Here are my typing and shorthand certificates.

Mr Watts: Good. Have you any other (d) _____? Can you use a computer?

Valerie: No, but I speak French and Spanish.

Mr Watts: Good. Your teachers tell us you're very careful and you get on well with other people, so there's no problem about your (e) _____. In fact you seem very suitable.

Valerie: Thank you. Can I just make sure of one or two points? I believe the (f) _____ are £150 a week. Is that right?

Mr Watts: Yes, that's right. And the (g) _____ are nine to five, Monday to Friday. Well, we'd like to have you, Miss Woods.

Valerie: Thank you very much. I think the job will suit me very well.

3 Finish each sentence on the left with the correct phrase on the right.

(a) He found   (1) in his work.
(b) He was   (2) an advertisement.
(c) He applied   (3) his work very interesting.
(d) He answered   (4) at science and mathematics.
(e) He had   (5) honest and hard-working.
(f) He was interested (6) to the company for a job.
(g) He was very good (7) a lot of experience.

4   Match each job in the following list with the correct picture.

scientist	waiter	porter	businessman	journalist
librarian	priest	lawyer	carpenter	labourer
secretary	farmer	actress	mechanic	footballer

5   We often use the following adjectives to describe different kinds of jobs.
Using a dictionary to find the meanings if necessary, give one or two
examples of jobs from Exercise 4 for each adjective.
E.g. badly-paid (with low wages or salary): labourer, porter

(a)   interesting   (d)   physically hard
(b)   boring   (e)   exciting
(c)   mentally hard   (f)   well-paid

6   Describe
(a)   a job that you have had
(b)   the job you have now
(c)   the job that you would like to have in the future

Education

1   Put each of the following words in the correct space in the passage below.

staff	primary school	pupils	learn	start
terms	play-school	compulsory	mixed	

Bobby's parents decided to send him to a (a) _____ when he was three. They wanted him to (b) _____ to play with other children. In Britain children must, by law, (c) _____ school at the age of five. Education is (d) _____ from then. Bobby's first real school was the (e) _____. There are three (f) _____ a year and holidays at Christmas, Easter and in summer. The (g) _____ are boys and girls together, so it's a (h) _____ school. The teachers on the (i) _____ are young and friendly. Bobby likes the school.

2   Instructions as above.

secondary school	take	specialise	state school	pass
private school	fail	subjects	marks	

Sally has just started her new school at the age of 11. There are different kinds of school from this age, but the general term for them is (a) _____. Sally's school is a government school, usually called a (b) _____. Some parents pay to send their children to a (c) _____. At first Sally will take a lot of different (d) _____ (history, English, chemistry etc.) but, after a few years, she'll begin to (e) _____ in things she is good at and interested in. Then she'll (f) _____ some exams. If she can (g) _____ a number of exams with good (h) _____ (A,B,C), it will help her to get a good job. Of course she hopes she doesn't (i) _____.

3   Instructions as above.

courses	last	degree	studies	graduate
grant	student	keen	fees	

Harry is 21. He passed his school exams with good marks and left school at 19. Now he's at university. He's a (a) _____ and he receives a (b) _____ from the state to help him pay the university (c) _____ and his personal expenses. He is very (d) _____ on his subject, mathematics, and it will be useful to him in the future. He works hard and enjoys his (e) _____. University (f) _____ in Britain usually (g) _____ for three years. After this, Harry hopes to (h) _____. A good (i) _____ will get him a good job.

4   Instructions as above.

mark	strict	graduate	prepare	teacher training college
behave	lessons	homework	classes

Jo is a teacher of English in a state secondary school. She's a (a) _____ of Sussex University with a degree in English Literature. When she graduated, she first worked in an office but was bad at typing and soon got bored with the job. She decided to teach, so she went to a (b) _____. Jo,teaches six different (c) _____ of children between the ages of 12 and 18. The pupils enjoy her (d) _____, but she finds it hard work. She gives the children a lot of (e) _____ to do, and every evening she has to (f) _____ it and (g) _____ for the next day. One problem is that the children in Jo's school don't (h) _____ very well. They're often impolite. Jo and the other teachers have to be very (i) _____ with them.

5   Put the correct word from the following list in each space below.

from   in   with   between   of   at   to   on

(a)   Bobby started school _____ the age of five.
(b)   They have a holiday _____ Christmas.
(c)   There's a holiday _____ the summer, too.
(d)   The teachers _____ the staff are very young.
(e)   Sally goes _____ a secondary school.
(f)   She'll probably pass _____ good marks.
(g)   Harry's _____ university.
(h)   He gets a grant _____ the state.
(i)   Mathematics will be very useful _____ him _____ the future.
(j)   Betty's a teacher _____ English.
(k)   She's a graduate _____ Sussex University.
(l)   She has a degree _____ English Literature.
(m) Her pupils are _____ 12 and 18.
(n)   She's very strict _____ them.

6   Use complete sentences to say what school subjects you are, or were
good at   bad at   interested in   bored with   keen on

You can choose from the following list of subjects, using a dictionary if
necessary to find the meanings.

biology	**art**	**history**	**literature**
mathematics	**chemistry**	**languages**	**computers**
sport	**physics**	**geography**	

7   Use complete sentences to answer the following questions about schools
in your country and your own education.
(a)   Do children usually go to play-schools? Are they free?
(b)   Between what ages is education compulsory?
(c)   When do you have holidays?
(d)   How long are they?
(e)   What different kinds of secondary schools are there?
(f)   Are they mixed schools?
(g)   Are there many private schools?
(h)   Did you specialise in certain subjects at school? Which ones?
(i)   Did you take any exams? What were the results?
(j)   What did you do, or what would you like to do, at university?
(k)   How long do university courses last?
(l)   Do students receive grants?
(m) Do you have to be a graduate to teach in a state school?
(n)   Did you do, or do you do, a lot of homework at school?
(o)   Do pupils behave well at school?

Money

1 Put each of the following verbs in the correct space in the passage.

pay back	spend	save	open	lend
borrow	earn	afford	owe	pay

Joy: Pam, I'm in trouble. I (a) _____ £200 a week from my job, but I need to (b) _____ about £250 a week just on basic things like food, rent and fares. I can't make ends meet on £200. I've got to (c) _____ some money. Can you help?

Pam: Yes, OK. I'm quite well-off at the moment. I can (d) _____ you £100. Here you are. But why don't you (e) _____ a bank account? It's very simple. Then you can (f) _____ a little bit every week, and you won't be so hard-up.

Joy: Pam, I haven't got enough money to put in a bank account! I can't (g) _____ my gas and electricity bills. I can't (h) _____ to go on holiday. I'm not just a bit hard-up. I've got no money at all. I'm broke! Anyway, thanks for your help. I promise to (i) _____ the £100 next month. I don't like to be in debt. I won't forget. I now (j) _____ you £100.

2 Put each of the following words or phrases in the correct space in the sentences below.

broke   **hard-up**   **in debt**   **well-off**   **make ends meet**

(a) She earns a lot of money. She's very _____.
(b) He never has a lot of money. He can't afford luxuries. He's always _____.
(c) I'll have to get an extra job in the evenings. I can't _____ on my salary.
(d) I'm sorry I can't lend you any money. I haven't got any. I'm absolutely _____.
(e) He's _____. He owes money to me and to the bank too.

3 Put the correct word from the following list in each space below.

in   **from**   **on**

(a) He earns £150 _____ his evening job.
(b) I spend £8 a week _____ fares.
(c) She has to make ends meet _____ £500 a month.
(d) I put some money _____ my bank account.

4 First match each item on the left below with its meaning on the right. Then divide the words into two groups under the headings 'Income' (money you receive) and 'Expenditure' (money you spend).

(a) **taxes**
(b) **pocket-money**
(c) **salary**
(d) **entertainment**
(e) **rent**
(f) **interest**
(g) **wages**
(h) **pension**
(i) **fares**
(j) **gas and electricity bills**

(1) cinema, theatre, restaurant meals etc.
(2) money for transport, e.g. bus, train, taxi
(3) part of income paid to government
(4) money parents give children every week
(5) money from work, usually hourly or weekly
(6) money for lighting, heating in your house
(7) money from work, usually monthly or annually
(8) e.g. 6% a year from your money in the bank
(9) money for people who stop work at the age of about 60
(10) weekly or monthly payments for your room, flat or house

5 Can you think of any more items of income or expenditure?

6   Answer the following questions using complete sentences.

(a)   What do you spend your money on?
(b)   How much does a doctor earn in your country?
(c)   Do you save any money? If so, how (bank, cash)?
(d)   Is it easy to open a bank account in your country? How much do you need to start?
(e)   Do you owe money? Who to? When will you pay back the money?
(f)   Is there something you want to do but can't afford to?
(g)   Do you often lend money? Who do you lend it to?
(h)   Do you often borrow money? Who do you borrow it from?
(i)   Do people in your country receive a state pension when they are old?
       How old are they when they begin to receive it?
(j)   What bills do you have to pay?
(k)   How much pocket-money did you receive when you were 12 years old?
(l)   In your country, what percentage of a person's income is taken in taxes?

A Life

1   Put each of the following verbs in the correct space in the passage.

bring up	**leave**	**settle down**	**educate**	**move**
was born	**join**	**come from**	**grow up**	**become**

Interviewer: Freddie, you're Scotland's number one footballer. Tell us about your early life. Where were you born?

Freddie Fox: Well, I (a) _____ in the North of Scotland 22 years ago. I (b) _____ a small, quiet village. It was a nice place for a child to (c) _____ and in the future I'd like to (d) _____ my own children in the country.

Interviewer: And where did you go to school?

Freddie Fox: Well, education is sometimes a problem in the country. My parents couldn't (e) _____ me themselves so I had to travel several miles to the nearest school. But then my father had to (f) _____ to Glasgow for his work.

Interviewer: And you were invited to (g) _____ Rangers Football Club.

Freddie Fox: That's right. I was 16 so I was able to (h) _____ school and (i) _____ a professional footballer.

Interviewer: And what about the future?

Freddie Fox: Well, I don't know. I'm still young. I'll get married. I'll play football as long as I can. When I stop, I hope to get a job as a club manager. And finally I'd like to (j) _____ in the North of Scotland again.

2   Put the correct word from the following list in each space below.

as   in   at   from

(a)   He's _____ the army.
(b)   He was born _____ South Wales.
(c)   I come _____ Sydney, Australia.
(d)   _____ the future I'd like to be a doctor.
(e)   I live _____ the country, not the town.
(f)   _____ the moment I'm a secretary.
(g)   I'll leave my job _____ a few years.
(h)   She wants to get a job _____ a nurse.

3   Finish each sentence on the left with the correct phrase on the right.
(a) To be a soldier   (1) you join the fire-brigade.
(b) To be a sailor   (2) you join the post office.
(c) To be a fireman   (3) you join the civil service.
(d) To be a policeman or policewoman   (4) you join the army.
(e) To be a postman   (5) you join the navy.
(f) To be a civil servant (in a government office) (6) you join the police force.

4   Answer the following questions about yourself using complete sentences.
You can sometimes use the phrases 'in 1978' or 'when I was 17' etc.
(a) Where do you come from? (village, town, region or country)
(b) Where were you born?
(c) Who were you brought up by?
(d) Where did you grow up?
(e) Did your family move? If so, where to?
(f) Where were you educated?
(g) When did you start school?
(h) When did you leave school? Or when will you leave school?
(i) When did you get married? Or when would you like to get married?
(j) What did you do when you left school? Or what will you do when you
     leave school?
(k) What would you like to do in the future?
(l) Where would you like to settle down?

5   Using words from the exercises above (with verbs in the past tense)
describe the lives of the following people.

(a)
	Yoko Tanaka
1964	Born Tokyo, Japan
1967	Parents died, lived with aunt
1970–82	School
1975	Aunt moved to Kyoto with Yoko
1982–86	Kyoto University
1986-	Civil Servant

(b)
	Oscar Gonzalez
1937	Born Madrid, Spain, lived with parents
1942–53	School
1953–65	Navy
1965–75	Police force (in Madrid)
1975	Married
1975–	Security guard (in Barcelona)

6   Describe your own life.

Sport

1 Match each word on the left below with the correct phrase on the right.

(a) **team**   (1) someone who plays a sport, e.g. a footballer
(b) **player**   (2) number of goals or points each player or team has
(c) **amateur**   (3) group of sportsmen who play together, e.g. eleven footballers
(d) **professional**   (4) person who controls a game
(e) **spectator**   (5) someone who plays a sport as a paid job
(f) **crowd**   (6) game, e.g. of football
(g) **referee**   (7) someone who plays a sport only for enjoyment, not money
(h) **match**   (8) group of people who watch a sporting event
(i) **score**   (9) person who watches a sporting event

2 Put each of the following verbs in the correct space in the passage.

win   lose   draw   train   beat   play   score

I love football. I don't just like to watch it. I like to (a) _____, too. I belong to a
team. Of course it's not my job. We're just amateurs, not professionals. Not many
people come to watch. We just have a small crowd. In fact, there are sometimes
more players than spectators! We have a game every Saturday, but we (b) _____
together every Tuesday and Thursday evening to prepare and keep fit. We're quite a
good team. We (c) _____ most matches. We only (d) _____ a few, and
sometimes we (e) _____ (for example, last Saturday the score was 2:2). Next
Saturday our match is against a very good team, but I think we'll (f) _____ them,
and if I'm lucky I'll (g) _____ a goal or two. Oh, we have a problem. Do you know
much about football? Would you like to run up and down in a black shirt and
shorts? Our referee has broken his leg. Would you like a job?

3 In most sports, a score of 0 (zero) is called 'nil', but in tennis and
table-tennis it's called 'love'. A score of 1:1, 2:2 etc. (a 'draw') is called 'one
all', 'two all' etc. How do we say the following scores?

football   **tennis/table tennis**
(a) 2:0   (d) 30:0
(b) 4:4   (e) 15:15
(c) 0:0   (f) 0:15

British and American English 1

There are not many differences between British and American English in the
written form. Here are some vocabulary differences.

British	American		British	American
autumn	fall		to post	to mail
film	movie		queue	line
flat	apartment		shop	store
lift	elevator		sweets	candy
pavement	sidewalk		timetable	schedule
petrol	gas		trousers	pants

4   Match each of the following sports with the correct picture below.

skiing	cycling	basketball	boxing	horse-riding
shooting	volley-ball	badminton	tennis	baseball
hockey	table-tennis	cricket	fishing	golf
skating	motor-racing	running	swimming	rugby
football				

5   Can you find the following sporting items in the pictures above?

(1) **boxing glove**   (11) **cricket bat**   (21) **football**
(2) **running track**   (12) **helmet**   (22) **baseball glove**
(3) **racing car**   (13) **baseball bat**   (23) **net**
(4) **pistol**   (14) **baseball cap**   (24) **swimsuit**
(5) **skis**   (15) **skate**   (25) **badminton racket**
(6) **shuttlecock**   (16) **target**   (26) **golf club**
(7) **basketball**   (17) **goal**   (27) **rugby ball**
(8) **running shoe**   (18) **hockey stick**   (28) **basket**
(9) **horse**   (19) **fishing rod**   (29) **boxing ring**
(10) **goggles**   (20) **tennis racket**   (30) **bicycle**

6   Which sport do you like best, and why?

Free Time and Holidays

In each space (a) in the three passages below put the word from the following group (a) which best suits the person in the picture. Then do the same for (b), (c) etc.

(a)   cultural things/parties/the open air
(b)   sociable/serious/active
(c)   classical music/sport/dancing
(d)   meeting people/nature/reading
(e)   concerts/clubs/sporting events
(f)   libraries/the countryside/discos
(g)   go by plane/hitch-hike/take a train
(h)   hotel/youth hostels/camp sites
(i)   learn about other countries/have a good time/be close to nature
(j)   sunbathe/go for walks/visit historical places

1   I love (a) _____. People say I'm (b) _____. I like (c) _____ and (d) _____ so I often go to (e) _____ and (f) _____. On holiday I (g) _____ and stay at a nice (h) _____ in Spain. I want to (i) _____. Every day I (j) _____ on the beach.

2   I'm keen on (a) _____. I'm a bit (b) _____. My hobbies are (c) _____ and (d) _____ so I spend a lot of time at (e) _____ and (f) _____. Holidays? Well, I usually (g) _____ to save money and stay at (h) _____ abroad because I want to (i) _____. I (j) _____ there.

3   I'm very fond of (a) _____. I'm a very (b) _____ person. I enjoy (c) _____ and (d) _____ so I love all (e) _____ and also (f) _____. Every summer my friends and I (g) _____ somewhere and sleep in our tents at (h) _____. We prefer to (i) _____. We (j) _____.

Learning Tips

Carry a small notebook with you everywhere. You can:

1 keep your new words alphabetically.
2 divide them into nouns, verbs, adjectives etc.
3 keep them by topics (street, nature, art etc.)
4 add a translation if you want to.

4   Put the correct word from the following list in each space below.

on   at   to   by   of   about

(a) I often go _____ discos and parties.
(b) We stayed _____ a cheap hotel.
(c) She sunbathes _____ the beach.
(d) I'm very keen _____ music.
(e) I spend a lot of time _____ concerts.
(f) I often go _____ concerts.
(g) He stays _____ youth hostels.
(h) He wants to learn _____ other countries.
(i) I'm very fond _____ the open air.
(j) We stayed _____ a camp-site.
(k) They prefer to live close _____ nature.
(l) I'm going there _____ plane.

5   Fill in the table to show the advantages of different types of transport and accommodation. The first one is done for you as an example.
(Note: you can use one tick or two.)

	Transport					Accommodation				
	hitch-hiking	going by car	going by coach	going by train	going by plane	luxury hotel	cheap hotel	youth hostel	camp-site	staying with friends
It's cheap.	✓✓									
It's comfortable.										
You feel free to do as you like.	✓									
It's interesting.	✓									
No need to plan or book.	✓✓									
No language problems abroad.										
It's quick.										
It's safe, not dangerous.										

6   Say what you think of the free-time activities on the right below, using the phrases on the left.

I love
I'm (not) interested in
I (don't) like
I'm (not) keen on
I (don't) enjoy
I get bored with

shopping.
window-shopping.
visiting museums and art galleries.
visiting historical places.
being in the countryside.
swimming and sunbathing.
going for walks.
meeting people.
eating and drinking.
collecting stamps, postcards etc.
cooking at home.
watching television.

7   Using words and phrases from the exercises above, describe how you spend (a) your free time when you don't go away and (b) your holidays.

Illness and the Doctor

1 Match each of the following words with the correct item in the picture.

doctor   **patient**   **nurse**   **receptionist**   **lungs**
brain   **stomach**   **heart**   **chemist**

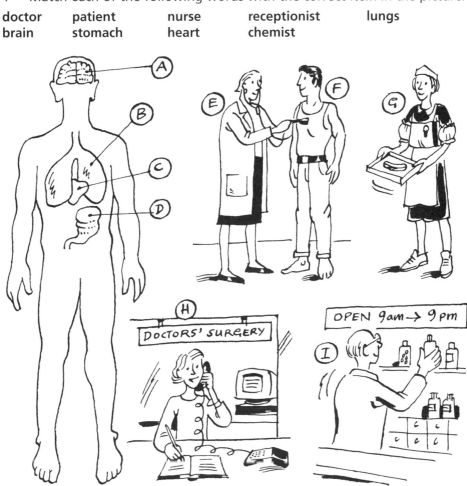

2 Put each of the following words or phrases in the correct space in the passage below.

look after   **treat**   **ache**   **examine**
suffer   **keep**   **cure**   **operate**

I am a family doctor. I have a nurse to help me and a receptionist to help the patients when they come to see me. When I see patients in my surgery, first I listen to their problems, then I (a) _____ them. Then, if I can, I (b) _____ them for their illnesses. Some simply have sore throats, headaches or flu and I give them a prescription to take to the chemist. Others (c) _____ from serious diseases of the heart, lungs, stomach or even brain. I can't always (d) _____ them myself and sometimes I have to send them to hospital for treatment. If something is seriously wrong with them, the hospital will decide to (e) _____ on them. The trouble is people don't (f) _____ themselves properly. It really isn't so difficult to (g) _____ well. If your head begins to (h) _____, have a rest. If you always feel tired, get more exercise. Eat well. Have a good diet. And have a regular check-up with the doctor.

3   Put the correct word from the following list in each space below.

for   on   in   with   to

(a) I saw the doctor _____ her surgery.
(b) She listened _____ my problems.
(c) They treated me _____ a heart problem.
(d) I took the prescription _____ the chemist.
(e) I had to go _____ hospital for an operation.
(f) Something's wrong _____ my back, doctor.
(g) They operated _____ him immediately.

4   For each sentence on the left below, find the correct meaning on the right.

(a) She **got a hearing-aid**.   (1) She couldn't see things far away.
(b) She **had no appetite**.   (2) Her head hurt.
(c) She **was a bit deaf**.   (3) She didn't want to eat anything.
(d) She **was short-sighted**.   (4) She bought something to help her hear better.
(e) She **went on a diet.**   (5) She rested.
(f) She **had a headache**.   (6) She couldn't hear very clearly.
(g) She **cut down on** cigarettes.   (7) She decided to eat and drink only certain things.
(h) She **took it easy**.   (8) She smoked less.

5   What advice would you give to a friend with the problems on the left?
For each one, choose one or more items from the right.

(a) I've cut my finger badly.   (1) Go and see a doctor.
(b) I think I've broken my leg.   (2) Take a day or two off work.
(c) I'm always tired.   (3) You'll probably need an X-ray.
(d) I'm smoking too much.   (4) Why don't you have your eyes tested?
(e) I've got flu.   (5) You should go on a diet.
(f) I'm getting a bit short-sighted.   (6) The chemist will be able to give
                                                 you something for it.
(g) I'm going deaf.   (7) Well, you'd better cut down.
(h) I'm getting fat.   (8) You might need a hearing-aid.
(i) There's something wrong with my heart. (9) Just take it easy for a few days.
(j) I'm drinking too much.   (10) Go to bed for a few days.
(k) I've lost my appetite.   (11) You should see a specialist.
(l) I've got a headache.   (12) You need more exercise.
(m) I'm sleeping badly.   (13) You may need an operation.

6   Describe your own health and any health problems you have.

In the Morning

1 Match each of the following words with the correct picture.

briefcase	shower	toothbrush	soap
teeth	hairbrush	newspaper	alarm clock
comb	clothes	pyjamas	electric razor

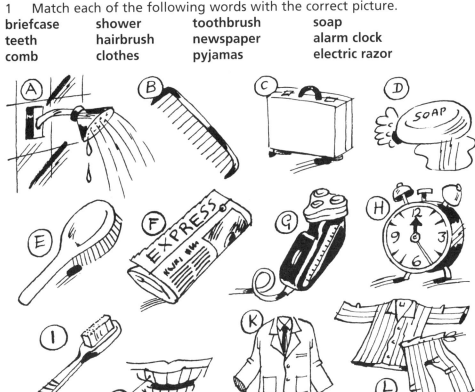

2 The following sentences are what people usually do in the morning. Put them in the right order, i.e. what we do first, what we do next, what we do after that, etc.

(a) I go into the bathroom.

(b) I turn off my alarm-clock.

(c) I get up.

(d) I sleep very heavily.

(e) I dress.

(f) My alarm clock goes off.

(g) I go into the kitchen.

(h) I wake up.

(i) I have my breakfast.

(j) I lie in bed for another ten minutes.

(k) I brush my teeth and comb my hair.

(l) I buy a newspaper.

(m) I catch a bus to work.

(n) I make my breakfast.

(o) I take my briefcase.

(p) I leave the house.

(q) I make my bed.

(r) I have a shower.

3   Put the correct verb from the following list in each sentence below.

dress   **put on**   **wear**

He's dressing.

He's putting on his shirt.

He's wearing a suit.

(a)   Policemen _____ uniforms so everyone knows who they are.
(b)   It's cold. I think I'll _____ a pullover before I go out.
(c)   I always _____ very quickly in the morning.
(d)   William is only a baby. His mother has to _____ his shoes for him.
(e)   At a wedding, people usually _____ their best clothes.
(f)   After I get out of the swimming pool, I dry myself, _____ and go home.

4   Describe how you get up (a) on weekdays (working days) and (b) at weekends and on holiday.

Collective Nouns

Collective nouns are groups, especially of people.
e.g.   team   family   government   class
       army   company   committee   BBC

If we think of the group as one thing, we use the singular.
    The team **is** very good. **It is** the best.
    The family **is** the smallest unit in society. **It is**…

If we think of it as different people, we use the plural.
    The team **are** getting on the bus. **They are** tired.
    The family **are** talking and drinking tea. **They are** …

The Telephone

1 Match each verb on the left with the correct phrase on the right.

(a) **dial**   (1) wait
(b) **dial direct**   (2) ring a phone number
(c) **look up**   (3) phone a number yourself without using the operator
(d) **hold on**   (4) phone, call
(e) **ring**   (5) find information in a book

2 Match each word or phrase on the left below with the correct phrase on the right.

(a) **wrong number**   (1) busy (when someone is using the line you want)
(b) **directory**   (2) public phone box
(c) **directory enquiries**   (3) person who helps you make a phone call
(d) **off-peak**   (4) phone number you get by mistake
(e) **interference**   (5) service you phone if you want to find a phone number
(f) **engaged**   (6) book of phone numbers
(g) **long-distance**   (7) very far, opposite of 'local'
(h) **call-box**   (8) not so busy time (when phone calls are cheaper)
(i) **operator**   (9) bad sound which makes it difficult to hear
(j) **receiver**   (10) prices, charges
(k) **rates**   (11) part of the phone you speak into and listen to

3 Put each of the words on the left in exercise 2 above in the correct space in the conversation below.

Bill: Is that Jane?
Nell: This is 377 0211. There's no one called Joan here.
Bill: Sorry, I must have the (a) _____. Oh, just a moment, I want *Jane*, not Joan.
Nell: Oh sorry, yes. She's here. Hold on a moment.
Jane: Hello, this is Jane.
Bill: Hi, this is Bill. I tried to ring before, but the line was (b) _____.
Jane: Yes, I was talking to my mother in Australia.
Bill: Oh, a (c) _____ call. Was it expensive? The (d) _____ are very high, aren't they?
Jane: Only if you go through the (e) _____. It's quite cheap if you dial direct, especially if you phone during the (f) _____ period.
Bill: Was it a good line? Was it easy to hear?
Jane: It usually is, but today there was a lot of (g) _____.
Bill: I need some help, Jane. I tried to look up Amy's number in the (h) _____ but I couldn't find it.
Jane: I'm afraid I haven't got it. Why don't you call (i) _____?
Bill: I'm in the street, in a (j) _____, and I've got no more money.
Jane: But it's free. You just pick up the (k) _____, then you dial 142.
Bill: Oh yes, how stupid!

Watching Television

1 What do you usually see on different television programmes? Match each type of programme on the left below with the correct item on the right.
(a) **nature films**   (1) football, boxing, swimming etc.
(b) **quiz shows**   (2) life in different countries
(c) **news and current affairs**   (3) people trying to win prizes by answering questions
(d) **soap operas**   (4) advertisements for products
(e) **commercials**   (5) animals, fish, birds, flowers, plants etc.
(f) **travel films**   (6) information about what's happening in the world
(g) **comedies**   (7) jokes and funny situations
(h) **sport**   (8) information for pupils and students
(i) **educational programmes**   (9) story of the daily life of a family

2 Which of the programmes above do you like? Use the following words.

relaxing   exciting   amusing   interesting   useful   boring
E.g. I find nature films interesting.

3 Put the correct word or phrase from the following list into the sentences.

turn on   look up   plan   record   turn off   switch

(a) I _____ a programme if I don't like it.
(b) I _____ good programmes on my video-recorder.
(c) I _____ the television as soon as I get home.
(d) I _____ to another channel if I'm bored.
(e) I _____ my viewing very carefully.
(f) I _____ the times of the programmes in the newspaper.

4 Answer the following questions.
(a) What are your favourite types of programme?
(b) How do you watch television? (Do you plan carefully, record, watch everything?)
(c) How many hours television do you watch every day?
(d) What would you do without television?
(e) Is television good in your country?
(f) How many channels have you got in your country?
(g) What are the advantages and disadvantages of television?

British and American English 2

Here are some of the main differences between British and American spelling.

British	American		British	American
aeroplane	airplane		neighbour	neighbor
centre	center		practise	practice
colour	color		pyjamas	pajamas
favourite	favorite		theatre	theater
grey	gray		travel-ling,	travel-ing
metre	meter		-ler, -led	-er, -ed

How to Do Things

How to do the Washing Up

1   Match each of the following words with the correct item in the picture.

dishes **brush** **cupboard** **sink** **washing-up liquid**
sponge **cloth** **drawer** **tap** **draining-board**

2   Put each of the following verbs in the correct space in the instructions below.

dry **rinse** **turn off** **fill**
add **drain** **put away** **turn on**

1   First put all the dirty dishes in the sink.
2   _____ the tap and _____ the sink with warm water. Then _____ the tap.
3   Now _____ some washing-up liquid.
4   Wash everything in the soapy water with a special sponge or brush.
5   _____ everything in clean water.
6   Put everything on the draining-board to _____ for a few minutes.
7   Then _____ everything with a cloth.
8   Finally _____ all the clean, dry things in cupboards or drawers.

3   Do you wash the dishes like this or differently? Describe how *you* wash the dishes.

How to make an English Breakfast

1   Match each of the following words or phrases with the correct picture below.

bowl	jug	tea-bag	frying-pan	kettle	toaster
salt	pepper	teapot	table-cloth	napkin	glass

2   Put each of the following verbs in the correct space in the instructions below.

fry	boil	stir	clear away
add	pour	lay	spread

1   _____ the table (with the table-cloth, knives, forks, spoons, plates, glasses, napkins etc.)
2   To make tea, first _____ the water in a kettle.
3   Put a tea-bag in a cup and _____ the boiling water on it. (This is quicker than using a teapot.)
4   _____ milk (from a jug) and sugar (from a bowl), and _____ with a spoon.
5   Make some toast, using the toaster, and _____ butter on it.
6   _____ eggs and bacon in a frying-pan.
7   Put it on a plate with the toast, and eat it with a little salt and pepper.
8   When you've finished your breakfast, _____ all the breakfast things.

How to do Keep-fit Exercises

1   Put each of the following verbs in the correct space in the instructions.

move   **raise**   **lower**   **turn**   **hang**   **stand**

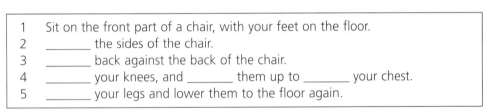

1	_____ with your feet apart. Let your arms _____ by your sides.
2	_____ your arms above your head.
3	_____ your body first to the left, then to the right. (Don't _____ your feet.)
4	_____ your arms to your sides again.

2   Instructions as above.

touch   **lean**   **hold**   **bend**   **bring**   **straighten**

1	Sit on the front part of a chair, with your feet on the floor.
2	_____ the sides of the chair.
3	_____ back against the back of the chair.
4	_____ your knees, and _____ them up to _____ your chest.
5	_____ your legs and lower them to the floor again.

3   Using words from the exercises above, give instructions how to do these exercises.

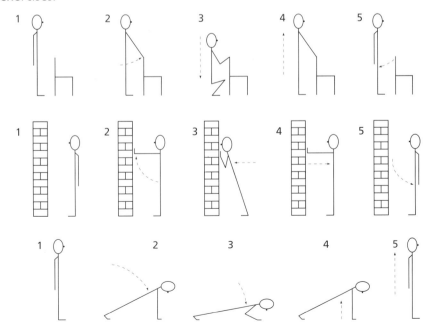

How to use a Radio/Cassette Player

1   Match each of the following words with the correct item in the picture.

plug	**buttons**	**batteries**	**point**
knob	**switch**	**controls**	**lead**

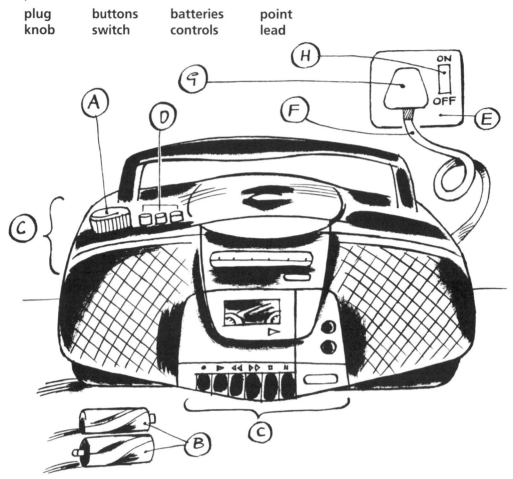

2   Put each of the following verbs in the correct space in the instructions below.

turn up	**press**	**unplug**	**switch on**
turn down	**turn**	**plug in**	**switch off**

1   First _____ at the nearest point.
2   Next _____ at the point.
    (The above will not be necessary if your machine is battery-operated)
3   Put a cassette in the machine and _____ the 'start' button.
4   To _____ the sound if it is too loud, _____ the 'volume' knob.
5   To _____ the sound if it is too low, turn the knob the other way.
6   You can adjust the quality of the sound by using the other controls.
7   When you have finished listening, press the 'stop' button.
8   Next _____ at the point.
9   Finally, _____ the machine.

Related Word Groups

Basic Adjectives

In the exercises below finish each sentence on the left with the best phrase on the right.

1

(a)	Glue is 5	(1)	**thin** and **straight**.
(b)	Jam is 3	(2)	**fragile** and **thin**.
(c)	A wine-glass is 2	(3)	**sweet** and **sticky**.
(d)	A pin is 4	(4)	**straight** and **sharp**.
(e)	A ruler is 1	(5)	**sticky** and **useful**.

2

(a)	A hammer is 3	(1)	**soft** and **cold**.
(b)	Snow is 1	(2)	**round** and **sweet**.
(c)	A pullover is 4	(3)	**hard** and **heavy**.
(d)	A cigarette is 5	(4)	**soft** and **warm**.
(e)	An apple is 2	(5)	**long** and **round**.

3

(a)	An elephant is 4	(1)	**expensive** and **powerful**.
(b)	The Atlantic Ocean is 5	(2)	**accurate** and **expensive**.
(c)	A Rolex watch is 2	(3)	**smooth** and **fragile**.
(d)	A Rolls Royce car is 1	(4)	**powerful** and **slow**.
(e)	A mirror is 3	(5)	**huge** and **deep**.

4

(a)	A comb is 5	(1)	**round** and **hot**.
(b)	Arnold Schwarzenegger is 4	(2)	**high** and **dangerous**.
(c)	Mount Everest is 2	(3)	**casual** and **useful**.
(d)	Jeans are 3	(4)	**wealthy** and **famous**.
(e)	The sun is 1	(5)	**cheap** and **light**.

5

(a)	A new baby is 3	(1)	**hot** and **dry**.
(b)	Fire is 5	(2)	**rough** and **dangerous**.
(c)	The Sahara Desert is 1	(3)	**tiny** and **weak**.
(d)	A stormy sea is 2	(4)	**calm** and **smooth**.
(e)	A quiet sea is 4	(5)	**hot** and **dangerous**.

6

(a)	A newspaper is 2	(1)	**high** and **famous**.
(b)	The Eiffel Tower is 1	(2)	**rectangular** and **useful**.
(c)	A motorway is 4	(3)	**strong** and **dangerous**.
(d)	A ball-point pen is 5	(4)	**long** and **wide**.
(e)	A tiger is 3	(5)	**useful** and **cheap**.

7 Use the above adjectives to describe each of the following.

(a) a cup 3,3
(b) a horse 2,4
(c) a cat 2,4
(d) a bottle 1,2
(e) chocolate 1,3
(f) a gun 3,1
(g) a passport 4,3 6,2

(h) an orange
(i) a pencil
(j) ice cream
(k) a millionaire
(l) a button
(m) a Boeing 747
(n) a sofa

(o) sugar
(p) a Sony Walkman
(q) a knife
(r) a plate
(s) a space rocket
(t) an overcoat

Basic Adjectives: opposites

In the exercises below replace each adjective with its opposite from the list above.

1 thick   fat   deep   hot   good   late

(a) It was a *bad* idea. 8 5
(b) He's very *thin*. 2
(c) The paper is *thin*. 1

(d) I took an *early* train. 6
(e) The water's very *shallow*. 3
(f) We had a *cold* meal. 4

2 casual   dark   heavy   major   new   young

(a) My luggage is *light*. 3
(b) It was a *light* evening. 2
(c) He's an *old* man. 6

(d) She wore *formal* clothes. 1
(e) It's a *minor* problem. 4
(f) It's an *old* book. 5

3 wide   wealthy   smooth   busy   calm   small

(a) It's a *big* room. 6
(b) What a *narrow* street! 1
(c) I've had a *quiet* day. 4

(d) They are a *poor* family. 2
(e) The wood was very *rough*. 3
(f) She felt *nervous* about her exam. 5

4 safe   short   blunt   public   wonderful   clean

(a) The knife's very *sharp*. 3
(b) It's a *dangerous* place. 1
(c) It was a *private* meeting. 4

(d) It was *terrible* news. 5
(e) He was wearing *dirty* clothes. 6
(f) The film was very *long*. 2

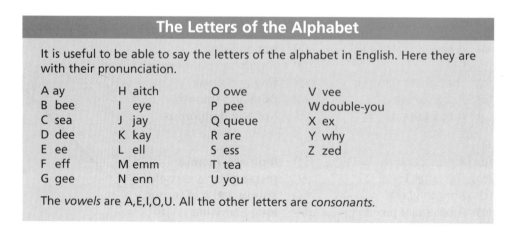

The Letters of the Alphabet

It is useful to be able to say the letters of the alphabet in English. Here they are with their pronunciation.

A ay	H aitch	O owe	V vee
B bee	I eye	P pee	W double-you
C sea	J jay	Q queue	X ex
D dee	K kay	R are	Y why
E ee	L ell	S ess	Z zed
F eff	M emm	T tea	
G gee	N enn	U you	

The *vowels* are A,E,I,O,U. All the other letters are *consonants*.

5   huge   easy   low   guilty   empty   tight

(a) The bottle is *full.*
(b) I am *innocent.*
(c) What a *difficult* question!
(d) It was a *tiny* animal.
(e) My belt is too *loose.*
(f) They are *high* buildings.

6   dry   cheap   weak   wrong   nice   slow

(a) It's a *fast* train.
(b) The weather was *nasty.*
(c) It was an *expensive* book.
(d) He gave the *right* answer.
(e) She's a *strong* woman.
(f) It was very *wet* weather.

7   soft   ugly   rude   stupid   sad   quiet

(a) He's an *intelligent* man.
(b) She feels very *happy.*
(c) He's a very *polite* boy.
(d) The chair was *hard.*
(e) They're *beautiful* buildings.
(f) The music was too *loud.*

Capital Letters

Capital letters are principally used for:

1 Proper nouns	Robert, Germany, Pacific Ocean, Tokyo
2 Titles before proper nouns	Mrs Brown, Uncle Fred, Dr Patel, King Juan Carlos, President Clinton
3 Words made from proper nouns	Shakespearean, German, English, Londoner
4 Certain dates and periods	Monday, April, Christmas, Ramadan (but *not* the seasons: spring, summer etc.)
5 First letter of a sentence or direct speech	He said, 'She doesn't love me.'
6 First person 'I'	I told him I was ill.
7 Beginning a letter	Dear Sir or Madam, …
8 Main words in titles of books, films etc.	*'A History of the Second World War'* (prepositions and articles usually have a small letter, unless they come at the beginning.)

Verbs

In each group below complete each sentence on the left with the correct phrase on the right.

1
(a) We **climb**   (1) pictures and maps.
(b) We **draw**   (2) eggs to make an omelette.
(c) We **weigh**   (3) songs.
(d) We **sing**   (4) mountains, stairs and ladders.
(e) We **break**   (5) ourselves, or a parcel before we send it.

2
(a) We **build**   (1) people if we make a noise.
(b) We **celebrate**   (2) our jackets or seat-belts.
(c) We **compare**   (3) a birthday or success by having a party.
(d) We **disturb**   (4) houses or walls.
(e) We **fasten**   (5) two or more things to see which is better, cheaper etc.

3
(a) We **feed**   (1) a picture on the wall or our jacket on a peg.
(b) We **fold**   (2) a person's age if we don't know it.
(c) We **guess**   (3) hungry animals and children.
(d) We **hang**   (4) a football with our feet.
(e) We **kick**   (5) our clothes when we pack, or a map when we've finished using it.

4
(a) We **knock**   (1) a cigarette, a candle or a fire.
(b) We **light**   (2) a nail into the wall with a hammer.
(c) We **mend**   (3) bicycles, motor-bikes or horses.
(d) We **punish**   (4) clothes which are torn or have holes in them.
(e) We **ride**   (5) people who do wrong by sending them to prison.

5
(a) We **repair**   (1) a problem if we can.
(b) We **rub**   (2) food and drink to see if it's good.
(c) We **shake**   (3) broken machines, old cars and parts of a house.
(d) We **solve**   (4) a bottle of medicine before we drink it.
(e) We **taste**   (5) our hands if it's very cold.

Formal Language

Formal language is the serious, careful language used in business letters, notices and regulations. Here are some formal words which we would not use in ordinary conversation.

state (say)	possess (have)	inform (tell)	terminate (finish)
request (ask)	require (need)	commence (begin)	infant (small child)
seek (want)	retain (keep)	depart (leave)	nation (country)

Action Verbs

1 Match each of the following words with the correct picture.

hairdresser   artist   driver   athlete   dressmaker   cleaner

Which of them do the following things?
(g) **cut, shampoo** and **comb**
(h) **dust, sweep** and **polish**
(i) **run, jump** and **throw**
(j) **measure, cut** and **sew**
(k) **draw, paint** and **sculpt**
(l) **accelerate, overtake** and **reverse**

2 Instructions as above.

pilot   teacher   dentist   postman   soldier   gardener

(g) **prepare, teach** and **mark**
(h) **collect, sort** and **deliver**
(i) **march, shoot** and **fight**
(j) **dig, plant** and **water**
(k) **take off, fly** and **land**
(l) **drill, fill** and **extract**

Adjectives Describing Character

In each sentence below put the correct adjective from the group of three above it.

1   impatient   sociable   adventurous

(a) She loves meeting people and going to parties. She's a very _____ person.
(b) She likes new things and new places, even if they're difficult or dangerous. She's _____.
(c) He gets very annoyed if he has to wait for anything. He doesn't like waiting. He's very _____.

2   ambitious   easy-going   talkative

(a) He never gets upset or annoyed when things go wrong. He's a very _____ man.
(b) He loves to talk to people and tell them what he thinks and what he's done. He's _____.
(c) She wants to get an important job in a high position. She's _____.

3   lazy   naughty   cheerful

(a) Little Rosie is always breaking things and doing what her mother tells her *not* to do. She's a _____ girl.
(b) He doesn't like work. He prefers to do nothing. He's _____.
(c) He's always happy and smiling. He's very _____.

4   sensible   selfish   optimistic

(a) She only thinks about herself. She doesn't care about other people. She's _____.
(b) He has a lot of common sense. He always knows the correct thing to do. He's a _____ boy.
(c) He always has good hopes for the future. He thinks everything will be fine. He's very _____.

5   polite   imaginative   tidy

(a) She's very careful about her appearance and how she arranges her desk and her room. She's a _____ young lady.
(b) He always remembers to say 'please' and 'thank you'. He's very _____.
(c) He has ideas like no one else's. He can write wonderful stories, draw unusual pictures and suggest unusual ideas. He's extremely _____.

6   For each of the 15 adjectives above find in the list below the best adjective which describes the *opposite* kind of person.

(a) **impolite**   (f) **sad**   (k) **bad-tempered**
(b) **hard-working**   (g) **well-behaved**   (l) **unambitious**
(c) **silly**   (h) **patient**   (m) **cautious**
(d) **pessimistic**   (i) **quiet**   (n) **unselfish**
(e) **unsociable**   (j) **untidy**   (o) **unimaginative**

People's Appearance

1   In each space (a) in the two descriptions of people below put the correct word from the following pair (a). Then do the same for (b), (c) etc.

(a) **short**
     strongly-built

(b) **in his thirties**
     elderly

(c) **straight**
     bald

(d) **glasses**
     bracelet

(e) **his arms folded**
     his hands on his hips

(f) **casually-dressed**
     formally-dressed

(g) **checked**
     striped

(h) **well-pressed**
     patched

(i) **well-polished shoes**
     trainers

He's a (a) _____, (b) _____ man. He's about 75 and he's (c) _____. He's wearing (d) _____ and he's standing with (e) _____. He's (f) _____ in a dark suit and a (g) _____ shirt. His trousers are (h) _____ and he's wearing (i) _____.

He's a (a) _____ man. He's probably (b) _____, maybe 34 or 35. He has dark, (c) _____ hair. He has a (d) _____ on his wrist and he's standing with (e) _____. He's (f) _____ in a (g) _____ shirt and (h) _____ jeans. He's wearing (i) _____.

2 Instructions as Exercise 1.

(a) **average height**
slim

(d) **bow**
necklace

(g) **plain**
spotted

(b) **middle-aged**
teenage

(e) **her hands by her sides**
her hands clasped

(h) **smart**
baggy

(c) **wavy**
curly

(f) **untidily-dressed**
neatly-dressed

(i) **high-heeled shoes**
sandals

She's a (a) _____, (b) _____ woman
of about 50. She has long, (c) _____
hair. She's wearing a (d) _____ and she
has (e) _____ in front of her.
She is (f) _____ in a black and white
(g) _____ blouse and a (h) _____
skirt. She's wearing black (i) _____.

She's (a) _____. She's a (b) _____
girl of, perhaps, 18. She has fair,
(c) _____ hair with a (d) _____
in it. She has (e) _____.
She's (f) _____. She's wearing a
dirty, (g) _____ tee-shirt, old,
(h) _____ trousers and a pair of
(i) _____.

3 Using the words and phrases from the above exercises, describe the people below.

Materials

1   Complete each sentence below, using the correct material from the following list.

metal   plastic   brick   wood   paper   denim   china   rubber
wool   stone   iron   steel   cotton glass   leather

(a)   Pullovers are made of _____.
(b)   A mirror is made of _____.
(c)   Books are made of _____.
(d)   Underwear (vests, pants) is often made of _____.
(e)   Jeans, and often jackets and skirts, are made of _____.
(f)   The Pyramids of Egypt are made of _____.
(g)   Shoes are usually made of _____.
(h)   Coins are made of _____.
(i)   Houses in Britain are often made of _____.
(j)   A cheap ruler is made of _____.
(k)   Doors are usually made of _____.
(l)   The Eiffel Tower in Paris is made of _____.
(m) Cutlery (knives, forks, spoons) is made of _____.
(n)   Crockery (plates, cups, saucers) is made of _____.
(o)   Car tyres are made of _____.

2   What are the following things made of?
cups, bottles, magazines, a watch, luggage, windows, envelopes, tables, a camera, jackets, typewriters, railway lines, Tower Bridge.

Geographical Words

1   Finish each sentence on the left with the correct phrase on the right.

(a)   Africa is   (1)   a city
(b)   Canada is   (2)   a river
(c)   Manchester is   (3)   a mountain
(d)   London is   (4)   a continent
(e)   Sicily is   (5)   a capital city
(f)   The Amazon is   (6)   a canal
(g)   Everest is   (7)   an ocean
(h)   The Himalayas are   (8)   a country
(i)   The Atlantic is   (9)   an island
(j)   The Mediterranean is   (10) a desert
(k)   The waterway across Panama between oceans is   (11) a mountain range
(l)   The Sahara is   (12) a sea

2   What are the following?
Holland, Bali, the Nile, Kilimanjaro, the Caribbean, Liverpool, Paris, the Andes, Suez, Europe, the Gobi, Malaysia, New York, Fuji, Cairo, Cyprus, Asia, the Mississippi, the Pacific, the Thames, Brazil.

Word Building

-ful and -less

It is sometimes *(but not always)* possible to make adjectives from nouns by putting *-ful* or *-less* on the end, e.g. 'careful' means '*with* care', 'careless' means '*without* care.'

Make a suitable adjective from the noun at the end of each sentence below by adding *-ful* or *-less* to the end.

(a)   Thank you for the books. They will be very _____ for my studies. (use)
(b)   This pen won't write at all. It's completely _____. (use)
(c)   Thanks to modern technology, a visit to the dentist is now often quite _____. (pain)
(d)   The policeman held my arms tightly behind my back. It was very _____. (pain)
(e)   The government is trying to help _____ families. (home)
(f)   Thank you for all you've done. You've been very _____. (help)
(g)   I'm very, very tired. I had a _____ night last night. (sleep)
(h)   We are _____ that the missing child will soon be found. (hope)
(i)   What is this food? It has no taste. It's _____. (taste)

'Interesting' and 'Interested' etc.

The *-ing* form of verbs, e.g. 'interesting', 'tiring', and the past participle, e.g. 'interested', 'tired', are often used as adjectives. The difference in meaning is seen in these sentences.
History was very *interesting* at school. I was very *interested* in it.
The journey was very *tiring*. We were very *tired* when we arrived.

Make the correct adjective, *-ing* form or past participle, from the verb at the end of each sentence.

(a)   It was a very _____ football match. (excite)
(b)   The children were very _____ on Christmas day. (excite)
(c)   We felt very _____ on holiday. (relax)
(d)   It was a wonderfully _____ holiday. (relax)
(e)   A shopkeeper likes to have _____ customers. (satisfy)
(f)   She was a nurse and found it a very _____ job. (satisfy)
(g)   It was a _____ film. I nearly fell asleep. (bore)
(h)   The book was very badly written. I soon got _____ with it. (bore)
(i)   After the explosion, the _____ children were taken to a safe place. (frighten)
(j)   A _____ noise woke me up in the middle of the night. (frighten)
(k)   He has an _____ habit of not looking at you when he's talking to you. (annoy)
(l)   We've had lots of complaints from _____ customers about our bad service. (annoy)

-er and -or

From an action verb we can sometimes make a noun ending -er or -or to describe the person who does the action, e.g. a 'player' is someone who plays (football, etc.), a 'conductor' is someone who conducts (an orchestra).
Make nouns ending -er or -or from these verbs.

(a) work
(b) visit
(c) clean
(d) act
(e) drive

(f) employ
(g) manage
(h) direct
(i) operate
(j) make

(k) paint
(l) build
(m) collect
(n) sail
(o) speak

(Note: sometimes there is a small change in spelling. e.g. swim-swimmer, law-lawyer, empire-emperor, and a small number of nouns end in -ar, e.g. lie-liar, beg-beggar)

-ist and -an

From a noun we can sometimes make another noun ending -ist or -an to describe a person connected with the noun, e.g. a 'tobacconist' is someone who sells tobacco, a 'Brazilian' is someone from Brazil.

From these nouns make other nouns ending -ist or -an describing people. (Note: there are sometimes small changes in spelling.)

(a) Christ
(b) typewriter
(c) politics
(d) America
(e) piano
(f) science

(g) electricity
(h) bicycle
(i) art
(j) guitar
(k) Rome
(l) novel

'Hourly', 'Daily' etc.

We can make adjectives from 'hour', 'day', 'week', fortnight' (two weeks), 'month' and 'year' by adding -ly to the end. Put each of the following words in its correct place in the sentences below.

hourly   daily   weekly   fortnightly   monthly   yearly

(a) The most famous British _____ newspaper is *The Times*.
(b) *Time* is an American _____ news magazine. I buy it every Tuesday.
(c) Her salary is £12,000 a year and she receives a _____ increase every September.
(d) He could possibly die in 24 hours. The doctors are giving him _____ tests to check his condition.
(e) She goes to see her parents every two weeks. They always look forward to these _____ visits.
(f) I haven't yet received my _____ salary cheque for February.

-en

1 We can often make a verb from an adjective (or sometimes a noun, e.g. 'length', 'strength') by adding -en to the end. 'To darken' means 'to make dark' or 'to become dark'.
E.g. He darkened his hair to change his appearance.
    The sky darkened as the clouds covered the sun.

In the spaces below put a verb ending -en made from the adjective or noun in brackets.

(a) Some screws in this machine are loose. I must _____ them. (tight)
(b) My belt is very tight and uncomfortable. I'll _____ it. (loose)
(c) Soon the dark clouds went away and the sky began to _____. (bright)
(d) This pencil isn't very sharp. It's blunt. I'll _____ it. (sharp)
(e) This noise is so loud it'll _____ me. (deaf)
(f) The river is quite narrow here, but as it gets near the sea it begins to _____. (wide)
(g) The runway is too short to take large, modern planes. They're going to _____ it. (length)
(h) The bridge is dangerous. It's not strong enough. There are plans to _____ it. (strength)

Number + Noun

Instead of saying 'a journey which took three hours', we can say 'a three-hour journey'. We have made a compound adjective by connecting the number and the noun, *which is used in the singular*. In the spaces below put similar compound adjectives made from the words in italics in the brackets.
E.g. He was wearing a _____ suit. (It cost *500 dollars*)
    He was wearing a *500-dollar* suit.

(a) We went on a _____ walk. (We went *five miles*)
(b) There will now be a _____ break. (It will last *ten minutes*)
(c) She's written a _____ book. (It has *200 pages*)
(d) It's a _____ hotel. (It has *20 storeys*)
(e) We had a _____ holiday. (It lasted *two weeks*)
(f) He's bought a _____ boat. (It's *ten metres* long)
(g) She's started a _____ English course. (It will last *six months*)
(h) The President will go on a _____ tour in April. (He'll visit *five countries*)
(i) He drives a _____ lorry. (It weighs *two tons*)

Colloquial Language

Colloquial language is the language used in informal conversation and letters to friends, but not in careful, formal speech and writing. Here are some examples.

hang on (wait)	paper (newspaper)	kid (child)
bike (bicycle)	no way (certainly not)	lots (much, many)
mum (mother)	take it easy (relax)	telly (television)
loo (toilet)	a get-together (a party)	bright (intelligent)

un-, dis-, in-, im-, il-, ir-

1 To give some words an opposite meaning, *un-* is put in front of them, e.g. She was very *unhappy.* Put *un-* in front of the following words and then put each word in its correct space below.

necessary **healthy** **well** **punctual**
employed **fair** **pleasant**

Vera: You look rather (a) _____. Why don't you see a doctor?
Alan: Oh no, that's (b) _____. I've just been working hard. I'm writing a book.
Vera: In this room? With the windows closed? And you smoke. That's very (c) _____. You'll be ill.
Alan: But if I open the windows, some very (d) _____ smells come in from the chemical factory.
Vera: And I hear you've been (e) _____ since you lost your job in the library.
Alan: Yes, they said I was (f) _____. But in fact I was only late a few times. It was very (g) _____.

2 Instructions as above.

satisfactory **friendly** **conscious** **usual** **hurt** **tidy** **successful**

(a) Just look at your room. It looks awful. It's so _____.
(b) He doesn't like the children in his new school. They're rather _____.
(c) I'm afraid your work is _____. You'll have to do better.
(d) It was an _____ film. I've never seen one like it.
(e) He hit his head on the door as he fell and was _____ for 20 minutes.
(f) I applied for the job but I was _____.
(g) Two people were injured in the accident but fortunately everyone else was _____.

3 Instructions as above.

dress **wrap** **tie** **lock** **do** **pack**

I like going away for a holiday but the best part is coming home again. I arrive home. I (a) _____ the door of my flat. I put my suitcase on the floor and start to (b) _____ it. I take out the things I have bought on holiday. I (c) _____ the string. I carefully (d) _____ them, look at them and put them on the table. I feel tired but very happy. I go into the bedroom. I (e) _____ my jacket and shoes. I take them off. I (f) _____ and I have a bath. I relax. I'm home again.

4 Put each of the following words in the correct space below. The words will be made opposite in meaning by the *dis-*, *in- im-*, *il-* or *ir-* already in the sentence.

convenient **polite** **formal** **honest**
regular **correct** **legal**

(a) I'm afraid the buses here are very ir_____. I sometimes have to wait an hour.
(b) This information is in _____. The train leaves at 3.20, not 3.10.
(c) The use of certain dangerous drugs is il_____. It's against the law.
(d) His house isn't near the shops, transport or his work. It's in a very in_____ place.
(e) She didn't say 'please' or 'thank you'. She was very im_____.
(f) It's not a special occasion. Just wear ordinary, in_____ clothes.
(g) She steals. She tells lies. She's completely dis_____.

Adverbs of Manner

Adverbs of manner tell us *how* something is done, e.g. She sings *beautifully*.
They also describe adjectives, e.g. She was *extremely* successful.
They are usually made from adjectives and usually end in '*-ly*':

slow-slowly   careful-carefully   dangerous-dangerously

Adjectives ending in *-y* usually drop the *-y* and add *-ily* to make the adverb:
happy-happily   lazy-lazily   sleepy-sleepily

Adjectives ending in *-ic* usually add *-ally* to make the adverb (but note:
public-publicly):
tragic-tragically   comic-comically   basic-basically

Some adjectives do not change as adverbs:
fast-fast   hard-hard   daily-daily   late-late

In the following sentences put in each space the adverb made from the
adjective in brackets.
(a)   I'm afraid I _____ forgot to bring my camera. (stupid)
(b)   It rained _____ for three hours. (continuous)
(c)   He died _____, trying to save his friend's life. (heroic)
(d)   The children were playing _____ in the garden. (noisy)
(e)   Please answer my questions _____. (truthful)
(f)   The film ended _____ with the hero's death in a gun-fight. (dramatic)
(g)   She worked very _____. (hard)
(h)   He looked _____ at the person who had interrupted. (angry)
(i)   She promised _____ that the government would not raise taxes. (public)
(j)   He's usually very lively, but today he's _____ quiet. (strange)
(k)   He arranged his desk very _____, everything in its right place. (tidy)
(l)   I agree with you _____. You're _____ right. (complete, absolute)

Verb Forms

Verbs normally have three main forms
       break, broke, broken

1 **break**   is the infinitive and present simple tense
       He began **to break** it.
       They **break** a lot of windows.

2 **broke**   is the past simple tense
       They **broke** a window yesterday.

3 **broken** is the past participle. It is used in perfect tenses, passives
       and sometimes as an adjective
       I have **broken** a window.
       A window has been **broken**.
       I noticed a **broken** window.

Compound Nouns

The important thing to remember in a compound noun (i.e. two nouns put together) is that the second noun is the real noun. The first is used like an adjective to describe what kind of thing or person the second noun is, e.g. a bedroom is a room with a bed in it.

There is no simple rule to tell you when the two parts of a compound noun are written together, with a hyphen or separately. You must learn the written form every time you learn a new compound noun, e.g. policeman, shoe-shop, railway station.

1 Make compound nouns from the following phrases.
E.g. a pot to make tea in: a teapot

(a) a party for someone's birthday
(b) a mark used after a question
(c) a library of a college
(d) a student at university
(e) furniture used in an office
(f) clothes we wear at work
(g) a driver of a lorry
(h) a programme on television
(i) a building used by the government
(j) a class held in the evening
(k) a window of a shop
(l) a knife for cutting bread

In a compound noun the first noun is usually in the singular. Make compound nouns from the following phrases.
E.g. a seller of flowers: a flower-seller

(m) a book to write exercises in
(n) an inspector of tickets
(o) a brush to keep your teeth clean
(p) an album you stick stamps in
(q) a map which shows roads
(r) a lace used for tying shoes
(s) juice from oranges
(t) a list of books
(u) a magazine about films
(v) a shop selling cameras
(w) a bus which carries tourists

2 When a compound noun is used in the plural, it is normally the second noun (the 'real' noun) which is made plural. The first one, like an adjective, remains singular. Make the following plural.
E.g. policeman – policemen; shoe-shop – shoe-shops; railway station – railway stations

(a) stamp collection
(b) city-centre
(c) teacup
(d) concert-hall
(e) family doctor
(f) picture-frame
(g) dog owner
(h) car-wheel
(i) airline pilot
(j) matchbox
(k) handbag
(l) garden chair

Idioms

Idiom is language where the words are not used with their usual, basic meanings. If you go to the theatre **once in a blue moon,** you go very rarely. If you haven't seen someone **for donkey's years,** you haven't seen him for a very long time. A large part of language is idiomatic. Here are some more examples.

She's **under the weather.** (feeling unwell)
I **got cold feet.** (scared)
He **dropped off.** (fell asleep)
We did it **in no time.** (very quickly)

I **turned in.** (went to bed)
She's **fed up.** (bored, annoyed)
Come at 6 **on the dot.** (punctually)
I'm **keen on** history. (like)

Word Forms

In each space in the exercises below put the correct word from the two or three above it.

1   decide (verb) decision (noun)
Will you take the job? We must have a quick _____. You must _____ very soon.

2   congratulate (verb) congratulations (noun)
I'd like to _____ you on passing your exam. Many _____!

3   permit (verb) permission (noun)
We cannot _____ children under 14 to go without their parents' _____.

4   invite (verb) invitation (noun)
Did we send the Smiths an _____ to our party? Did we _____ them?

5   arrive (verb) arrival (noun)
The _____ of the London train will be 15 minutes late. It will _____ at 10.45.

6   depart (verb) departure (noun)
The next train for Newcastle will _____ from platform 4. The _____.will
be in ten minutes

7   complain (verb) complaint (noun)
I think I'll _____ about this bad service. I'll make a _____.

8   argue (verb) argument (noun)
They don't get on well. They often _____. They're having an _____ now.

9   importance (noun) important (adjective)
It doesn't matter. It's of no _____. It's not _____.

10   difficulty (noun) difficult (adjective)
It's very _____ to operate this machine. I have great _____ in doing it.

11   height (noun) high (adjective)
What's the _____ of that mountain? How _____ is it?

12   arrange (verb) arrangement (noun)
I don't like the _____ of the furniture in this room. I think I'll _____ it differently.

13   bleed (verb) blood (noun)
If you don't do something about that cut, it'll _____ all over the place.
There'll be _____ everywhere.

14   practise (verb) practice (noun)
You need more English _____. You must _____ more.

15   describe (verb) description (noun)
I gave the police a _____ of the stolen goods. I had to _____ everything.

16   explain (verb) explanation (noun)
I'd like an _____ of your absence. Please _____ why you weren't at work
yesterday.

17   enjoy (verb) enjoyable (adjective)
I always have a good time at your parties. I always _____ them.
They're very _____.

18 fly (verb) **flight** (noun)
We _____ to Brazil on Thursday. Our _____ is at 10.45 a.m.

19 sign (verb) **signature** (noun)
I need your _____ on this paper, please. Could you _____ here?

20 meet (verb) **meeting** (noun)
I'm going to _____ some friends tomorrow. Our _____ is at two o'clock.

21 heat (noun) **hot** (adjective)
It's a very _____ country. The _____ is too much for me.

22 suit (verb) **suitable** (adjective)
What about six o'clock? Will that time _____ you? Will that be a _____ time?

23 relax (verb) **relaxation** (noun)
On holiday I don't like to do anything. I just want sun, sleep, food and _____.
I just want to take it easy and _____.

24 choose (verb) **choice** (noun).
I don't know which one to _____. It's difficult to make a _____.

25 legalise (verb) **legal** (adjective)
It isn't _____ to sell alcohol to children, and the government has no plans to
_____ it.

26 modernise (verb) **modern** (adjective)
My kitchen is very old. I'm going to _____ it. I've always wanted a _____
kitchen.

27 industry (noun) **industrial** (adjective)
Japan's _____ has made her rich. Japan is an _____ country.

28 agriculture (noun) **agricultural** (adjective)
This is an _____ area. There are no factories, only farms, only _____.

29 simplify (verb) **simple** (adjective)
This explanation is too complicated. Can you make it more _____?
Can you _____ it?

30 admit (verb) **admission** (noun)
This ticket will _____ one person free. It will give free _____.

31 freedom (noun) **free** (adjective)
The people demonstrated for more _____. They wanted to be _____.

32 weigh (verb) **weight** (noun)
I _____ 65 kilos. What's your _____?

33 noise (noun) **noisy** (adjective)
It's very _____ here. Where's the _____ coming from?

34 safety (noun) **safe** (adjective)
I'm worried about the children's _____. I hope they're _____.

35 danger (noun) **dangerous** (adjective)
The children can play here. It's not _____ at all. There's no _____.

36 peace (noun) **peaceful** (adjective)
You'll find all the _____ you want here. It's a very quiet, _____ place.

37 lose (verb) **loss** (noun)
If you _____ your money, you should tell the police about the _____ at once.

38 mix (verb) **mixture** (noun)
First _____ everything together and then put the _____ in a saucepan.

39 dirt (noun) **dirty** (adjective)
It was a very _____ place. There was _____ everywhere.

40 violence (noun) **violent** (adjective)
We live in _____ times. There are pictures of _____ in the newspapers every day.

41 measure (verb) **measurement** (noun)
How long is it? The _____ must be very exact. _____ it very carefully.

42 kindness (noun) **kind** (adjective)
She was very _____ to us. I thanked her for her _____.

43 happiness (noun) **happy** (adjective) **happily** (adverb)
(a) The children played _____ in the garden all morning.
(b) He has a good job and a lovely family. He's a very _____ man.
(c) Their children gave them a lot of _____.

44 succeed (verb) **success** (noun) **successful** (adjective)
(a) The film was a great _____. It made 75 million dollars.
(b) Do you think they will _____ in finishing the work this week?
(c) He was very _____ in his job and soon became Managing Director.

45 die (verb) **death** (noun) **dead** (adjective)
(a) If the doctor doesn't come soon, she'll _____.
(b) The police found a _____ body in the river.
(c) The _____ of the President was announced on television.

Similar Words

Be careful. The words in each of the following groups have exactly the same pronunciation.

your (of you)	Is that **your** car?
you're (you are)	**You're** late today.

weather (temperature, rain etc.)	The **weather** was sunny and warm.
whether (similar to 'if')	I don't know **whether** to go or not.

their (of them)	They took **their** coats.
they're (they are)	**They're** old friends.
there (other meanings)	**There's** a cat **there**.

passed	(verb)	He's **passed** the exam. I **passed** the shop.
past	(noun)	It happened in the **past**.
	(adjective)	The **past** tense is ...
	(preposition)	I walked **past** the shop.
	(adverb)	I walked **past**.

Idioms

Verb Phrases

1 Put each of the following phrases in the correct space in the conversation below.

make an appointment   **make a noise**   **make sure**
make your breakfast   **make a list**   **make your bed**

Mother: George, don't forget to (a) _____ and tidy your room. It's nine o'clock.
              I'm going shopping.
George: OK, Mum. Can you buy some things for me, please?
Mother: Yes, (b) _____ of the things you want and give it to me. Quickly.
George: OK. I've got to (c) _____ with the dentist. I've got toothache.
Mother: All right. I'm going out in two minutes. You'll have to (d) _____ yourself.
              There's plenty of bread and eggs and tea.
George: OK, Mum.
Mother: And (e) _____ you wash up afterwards! Don't forget.
George: All right. Here's the list of things I want. Thanks.
Mother: Right. And don't (f) _____ in the kitchen. Keep quiet. Remember your
              father's in bed with flu.

2 Put each of the following phrases in the correct space in the passage below.

make a decision   **make friends**   **make enquiries**
make some money   **make plans**   **make an effort**

To go and live abroad or not? It needs a lot of thought. After you (a) _____ to go,
you must organise yourself. First (b) _____ in your own country about
accommodation, language schools and work possibilities. You'll need this
information so that you can (c) _____. In the new country, perhaps it will be the
first time you've lived alone. Maybe you'll want to get a job to (d) _____ so you'll
have to look for work. You might feel lonely and you'll have to (e) _____ with
other young people. Sometimes this isn't easy in a big city. Well, it's up to you. You'll
have to (f) _____.

3 Put each of the following phrases in the correct space in the sentences.

take an exam   **take a seat**   **take place**
take a photo   **take any notice**   **take care**

(a)   This vase is very old and valuable. Please _____ when you clean it.
(b)   Look at that lovely old house. I think I'll _____ of it.
(c)   He's working very hard every evening. He's going to _____ next month.
(d)   Mr Jenkins will be here in a moment. Please _____.
(e)   I told him it was a dangerous machine, but he didn't _____. That's why he
        hurt his hand.
(f)   The meeting will _____ in the director's office at 11 a.m.

4 Put each of the following phrases in the correct space in the conversation below.

have a rest   **have a party**   **have a game of tennis**
have a bath   **have fun**   **have breakfast**

Jennie: What do you do on Saturdays?
Donald: Well, I get up late and (a) _____ or shower.
Jennie: Then you (b) _____?
Donald: Yes, bacon and eggs. Fruit juice. Then I usually (c) _____ in the park
            with a friend.
Jennie: Oh, are you good at tennis?
Donald: No, but we enjoy ourselves. We (d) _____.
Jennie: And in the evening?
Donald: Oh, I usually invite a few friends to my place and we (e) _____.
            You know, music, food, drinks, dancing.
Jennie: And on Sunday?
Donald: On Sunday I don't do anything. I just (f) _____.

5 Put each of the following phrases in the correct space in the sentences.

keep calm   **keep still**   **keep awake**
keep fit   **keep quiet**   **keep a record**

(a)   They _____ by walking, running and swimming every day.
(b)   I want to draw a picture of you. Don't move. _____.
(c)   Ladies and gentlemen, there is a small fire in the cinema. There's no need to
       worry. Please just _____ and leave by the exit doors.
(d)   Teachers must _____ of student attendance by filling in the class register
       every day.
(e)   I'm so tired I don't think I can _____ any longer.
(f)   The children are asleep so don't make a noise. _____.

6 Put each of the following phrases in the correct space in the passage.

do my shopping   **do me good**   **do a lot of harm**
do exercises   **do some work**   **do the housework**

I think I'm very well-organised. I (a) _____ at the supermarket every evening on my
way home from work. When I get home, I (b) _____ (cleaning, washing, tidying
up etc.). After dinner I (c) _____ I've brought home from the office. Before I go to
bed, I (d) _____ to keep in good condition. I think they (e) _____ because I'm
always fit and well. I don't smoke at all. I think cigarettes (f) _____.

7 Put each of the following phrases in the correct space in the sentences.

get a train   **get ready**   **get a lot of money**
get married   **get flu**

(a)   Jim and Rosemarie are going to _____ and I'm going to the wedding.
(b)   Nurses do a wonderful job but they don't _____.
(c)   If you don't put on more clothes in this cold weather, you'll _____.
(d)   The buses are very slow. Let's _____.
(e)   We're going out in five minutes, children. Hurry up. _____. Put your coats on.

'Touch'

Put each of the following phrases in the correct space in the passage.

get in touch   keep in touch   get out of touch

Well goodbye, Murray. I hope you have a good time in Africa. You've got my address, so please (a) _____. Write sometimes. It would be a pity to (b) _____. Oh, have you got Ann's address? I don't know where she is. I want to (c) _____ with her to ask her to a party.

Prepositional Phrases

1   Put each of the following phrases in the correct space in the passage.

at school   at work   at once   at least
at the seaside   at home   at last   at first

I'll always remember that day. I was 15. I had a bad cold and I was (a) _____ alone. My father was (b) _____ (he's a bus-driver). My older sister had gone to the coast for a day (c) _____. My 13-year-old brother was (d) _____. My mother was out shopping. I heard a strange noise. (e) _____ I thought it was my mother returning, but it wasn't the door. It was water! Rain? No, it wasn't raining. The kitchen taps? No, they were off. The bathroom? No. I thought and thought. It must have been (f) _____ ten minutes before I realised the noise came from the flat upstairs. (g) _____ I ran upstairs and knocked on Mr Black's door. No answer. I knocked again. And again. (h) _____ he came and opened it. He had turned on the water for a bath, forgotten all about it and fallen asleep in his chair.

2   Put each of the following phrases in the correct space in the conversation below.

on foot   on holiday   on the other hand   on fire
on time   on business   on second thoughts   on the one hand

Pam: Hi, Sue. Am I late? The traffic was terrible.
Sue: No, you're not late. It's exactly six o'clock. You're exactly (a) _____. What's the matter?
Pam: Firemen and fire-engines everywhere. There's a house (b) _____ near the cinema. I couldn't get a bus. I had to come (c) _____.
Sue: Well anyway, you're here. Liz can't come. She's in Italy.
Pam: Oh, is she (d) _____? Italy's lovely at this time of the year.
Sue: No, she had to go there (e) _____. She's gone to a meeting for her firm.
Pam: Well, where shall we go for *our* holiday? Spain? I don't know. (f) _____ Spain's always sunny in summer, but (g) _____ it's a bit crowded.
Sue: Yes, I thought of Spain too, but (h) _____ I think I'd prefer Holland.

3   Put each of the following phrases in the correct space in the sentences.

in prison   **in a hurry**   **in time**   **in trouble**
in love   **in person**   **in tears**   **in a mess**

(a)   You can't make a reservation by phone or post. You must do it _____.
(b)   She rang the police and they arrived just _____ to catch the burglar.
(c)   He spent six years _____ for the crime.
(d)   Please tidy up your room. It looks awful. It's really _____.
(e)   He's very difficult to control. He's always _____ at school.
(f)   Andrew's been very quiet recently. I think he's _____ with the new girl at the office.
(g)   The children were very shocked and upset by the sad news. Many of them were _____.
(h)   Sorry I can't stop and talk now. I'm _____.

4   Put each of the following phrases in the correct space in the conversation below.

by chance   **by all means**   **by bus**   **by post**
by phone   **by the way**   **by car**   **by mistake**

Jack: I've done something stupid. (a) _____ I told Sara I'd meet her tomorrow. I meant to say the day after tomorrow. Tomorrow I'm busy at the office.
Alex: Can't you contact her and explain?
Jack: That's the problem. A letter wouldn't reach her in time, so I can't let her know (b) _____. How can I tell her?
Alex: (c) _____, or don't you know her number?
Jack: She hasn't got a phone. Have you, (d) _____, got her neighbours' number? You know. The Smiths.
Alex: No, sorry. Why don't you drive to her flat now? You could get there in an hour (e) _____.
Jack: No, it's being repaired, and it would take ages to go (f) _____. Anyway, she's miles from a bus-route. Alex, do you think you could phone her at her office tomorrow morning?
Alex: (g) _____, of course. Good idea. (h) _____, when will your car be OK again? I was going to ask if I could borrow it on Saturday.

5   Put each of the following phrases in the correct space in the sentences.

out of doors   **out of control**   **out of date**
out of breath   **out of order**   **out of work**

(a)   This timetable's no good. It's last year's. It's _____.
(b)   He's very sunburnt and healthy. He spends a lot of time _____.
(c)   This telephone doesn't work. It's _____.
(d)   If the government doesn't do something very quickly, the situation will get _____.
(e)   He'd been running hard and arrived _____.
(f)   He's been _____ for four months, but he thinks he'll get a job soon.

Pairs

1   Put each of the following phrases in the correct space in the sentences.

more or less   **on and off**   **yes and no**   **so and so**

(a)   I've _____ finished the book. I've got two more pages to read.
(b)   In English, you begin a letter 'Dear _____'.
(c)   I've been learning English for six years _____. There were several breaks in that time, when I was too busy to study.
(d)   Do I like my new job? Well, _____. I'm not sure yet.

2   Instructions as above.

peace and quiet   **likes and dislikes**   **do's and don'ts**   **little by little**

(a)   Uncle Henry's coming to stay this weekend. What does he like to eat? Where will he want to go? Has he any particular _____?
(b)   At first I found the new job strange and difficult, but _____ I settled down.
(c)   The school is quite a relaxed place. It's not strict at all. There aren't many _____.
(d)   What a noisy, busy job this is. I'm looking forward to getting some _____ in the country this weekend.

Time

Put each of the following phrases in the correct space in the conversation.

one day   **from now on**   **ages**   **for good**   **the other day**   **so far**

Fiona: Hello, Sally. I haven't seen you for (a) _____. At least a year. How are you?
Sally: Hi, Fiona. I'm fine. I've just started a new business. We started (b) _____. In fact it was just last Thursday.
Fiona: Yes, I heard about it. And I've seen your shop. How's business?
Sally: Well, after only a few days I'm not sure. (c) _____ it's been good, but we sell swim-suits and the weather's been very sunny, but now it's turning cold so (d) _____ it might not be so good.
Fiona: What about you and Jimmy? Are you two married yet?
Sally: No, but probably in the future. I don't know when. (e) _____. What about you? You've been abroad a lot. Are you going away again?
Fiona: No, I've had enough travelling. I'm staying here (f) _____. Well, I've got to go. See you soon. I need a swim-suit.

'Mind'

Put each of the following phrases in the correct space in the conversation.

change your mind   **I don't mind**   **mind your head**
make up your mind   **on your mind**   **read your mind**

(a)   Tell me what's worrying you. What's _____?
(b)   I'm depending on you to help me tomorrow. I hope you don't _____.
(c)   You must decide soon. Come on, _____.
(d)   This door is very low so _____.
(e)   It doesn't matter if you come late. It's OK. _____.
(f)   I know what you're thinking. I can _____.

Things We Say

The exercises below give phrases often used in common situations. In each exercise find the best answer on the right to each phrase on the left.

1

(a) How do you do?
(b) How are you?
(c) Can you help me?
(d) I'm off.

(1) Bye. See you.
(2) Sure, no problem.
(3) I'm fine.
(4) How do you do?

2

(a) Hi!
(b) I've passed my exam!
(c) I've failed my exam.
(d) Where's Jack?

(1) Congratulations!
(2) Oh, hard luck.
(3) He's around somewhere.
(4) Hi!

3

(a) Thank you very much.
(b) I'm sorry I can't help you.
(c) Where's the post-office, please?
(d) Do you fancy coming to the cinema tonight?

(1) I'd love to.
(2) Sorry, I've no idea.
(3) Never mind. Thanks anyway.
(4) Not at all.

4

(a) What a nice flat you have.
(b) Are you hungry?
(c) What are you going to give me for my birthday?
(d) Come on. We're late.

(1) Wait and see.
(2) Yes, make yourself at home.
(3) Yes, I'm starving.
(4) Just a moment. Hang on.

Comparative and Superlative of Adjectives

There are two ways of making the comparative and superlative of adjectives.

1 If the adjective is short (one syllable), we usually add **-er** and **-est**
   I am **young**. You are **younger**. He is the **youngest**.

2 If the adjective is long (three syllables or more), we use **more** and **most**.
   This is **expensive**. That's **more expensive**. That's the **most expensive**.

3 Some adjectives of two syllables use the first form,
   e.g. **clever, cleverer, cleverest**

   Some use the second form,
   e.g. **careful, more careful, most careful**

   Some can use either,
   e.g. **simple, simpler, simplest** or **simple, more simple, most simple**.

4 Some adjectives are irregular,
   e.g. **good, better, best** and **bad, worse, worst**.

Miscellaneous

Abbreviations

1   Put each of the following abbreviations in the correct place in the note below, which Julie left for her flat-mate, Molly.

Abbreviation	Meaning	We say …
etc.	and so on *(et cetera)*	'and so on' or 'et cetera'
e.g.	for example *(exempli gratia)*	'for example' or 'for instance'
c/o	care of (in an address)	'care of'
a.m.	before noon *(ante meridiem)*	'a.m.'
p.m.	after noon *(post meridiem)*	'p.m.'
Rd	road (in an address)	'road'
PTO	Please Turn Over (at the bottom of a page)	'please turn over'
PS	after writing *(postscript)*	'PS'
US	United States of America	'US'

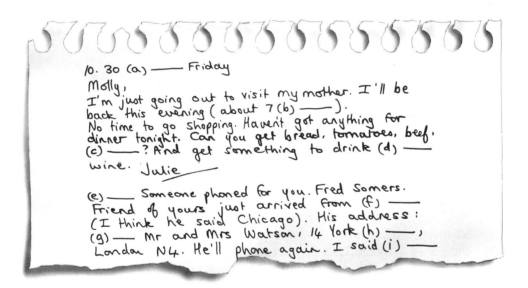

10. 30 (a) —— Friday

Molly,
I'm just going out to visit my mother. I'll be back this evening (about 7 (b) ——).
No time to go shopping. Haven't got anything for dinner tonight. Can you get bread, tomatoes, beef. (c) —— ? And get something to drink (d) —— wine. Julie

(e) —— Someone phoned for you. Fred Somers. Friend of yours just arrived from (f) —— (I think he said Chicago). His address: (g) —— Mr and Mrs Watson, 14 York (h) ——, London N4. He'll phone again. I said (i) ——

Regular and Irregular Verbs

1 Regular verbs make the past simple and past participle from the infinitive, and end in -*ed*
work, worked, worked

2 Some verbs have alternative forms.
learn, learned/learnt, learned/learnt

3 Irregular verb forms can be found in special lists in dictionaries and grammar books.
see, saw, seen

2   Put each of the following abbreviations in the correct place in the passage below.

Abbreviation	Meaning	We say …
BC	Before Christ	'BC' or 'Before Christ'
AD	After Christ (Anno Domini)	'AD' or 'After Christ'
i.e.	this means (id est)	'that is' or 'i.e.'
lb(s)	pound(s) weight (libra) (1 lb = 0.454 kg)	'pound(s)'
in(s) (")	inch(es) (1 in = 2.54 cm)	'inch(es)'
ft (')	foot/feet (1 ft = 0.3048 m)	'foot/feet'
UK	United Kingdom	'UK' or 'United Kingdom'
EU	European Union	'EU' or 'European Union'

The piece of stone is about 1 (a) _____ 9 (b) _____ long and weighs nearly 6 (c) _____. It bears the name of the Egyptian King Tutankhamen, who died over 3,000 years ago in 1343 (d) _____. It was discovered almost exactly 3,000 years after his death in 1655 (e) _____ and taken to Constantinople ((f) _____ the modern Istanbul). It will shortly go on a tour of museums in France, Italy, Spain, Germany and other (g) _____ countries, including, we hope, the (h) _____.

3   Read the following sentences as they would normally be spoken.
(a)   I work from 8.30 a.m. to 4 p.m. and do housework e.g. cleaning, washing etc.
(b)   His address is c/o Mrs L. Steel, 4 Dover Rd, Chicago, US.
(c)   At the bottom of his letter he writes, 'PS I'm going to Scotland next month,' then, 'PTO', and he gives his Scottish address on the back.
(d)   The average height of a man in the UK is 5ft 8 ins, i.e. about 173 centimetres.
(e)   Italy is a member of the EU.
(f)   A metal object 1'9" long of about 500 BC was found in the third century AD.

Reading Dates and Numbers

1   Write the following sentences as they would normally be written.
E.g. He paid one hundred and sixty pounds: He paid £160.

(a)   He died on the sixth of April seventeen forty-three.
(b)   They cost two pounds thirty-five pence.
(c)   My phone number is three seven oh double-four nine two.
(d)   There are one thousand two hundred and seventy-six people in the village.
(e)   One centimetre is nought point three nine three seven inches.

2   Read the following sentences as they would normally be spoken.
(a)   I was born on 4th May, 1937.
(b)   The tickets were £4.50 each.
(c)   Phone me on 408 9117.
(d)   The price is £12,750.
(e)   1lb = 0.454 kilograms.

Punctuation Marks

Match each of the following words or phrases with the correct punctuation mark below.

inverted commas   **apostrophe**   **hyphen**   **comma**   **small letter**
exclamation mark   **question mark**   **full stop**   **brackets**   **capital letter**

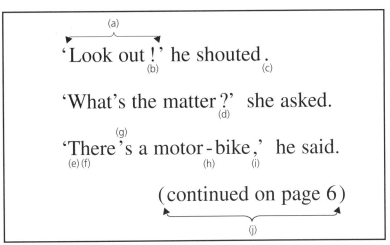

Punctuation

Full stops, question marks and exclamation marks

	name	purpose	examples
.	full stop	to mark the end of a sentence	He was here yesterday.
		after people's initials	F. L. Brown, W. Smith
		sometimes in abbreviations but often not used, especially when abbreviation has first and last letter of common word	Tues., Sept., U.K. or UK, B.B.C. or BBC, Mr, Mrs, Dr, Rd, St
?	question mark	to mark the end of a direct question	Where are you going? Is Bob here?
!	exclamation mark	to mark the end of an exclamation or strong command	He's dead! Good Lord! Get out! Be quiet! Help!

1   **Put in full stops, question marks and exclamation marks where necessary.**

(a)   We've received a letter from Mr A W Holden Have you seen it

(b)   He arrives on 17 Sept on BA flight 301 He'll stay in UK till the following Thurs before going to the USA, Japan and Australia What a journey Will Sue meet him at the airport

(c)   Go Get out Now It's dangerous Can't you see

(d)   She asked me if the US is in the EU What a question

(e)   What are you doing Are you going out Remember to take your key

Commas

	name	purpose	examples
,	comma	to mark a pause between words or phrases in a list, except where they are joined by 'and' or 'or'	It was red, green and white. I don't drink beer, wine or spirits She took out her key, opened the door and went in.
		round the name of a person spoken to	How are you, John? You know, Susan, this is serious.
		round 'yes' or 'no' used as answers	Yes, I know. No, I can't.
		round greetings etc.	Hello, how are you? Goodbye, I'm off. Dear Sir, Yours Truly,
		in addresses (especially if written on one line) and dates	4 Elm St, Woking, Surrey, England. 10th April, 1988

1 **Put in commas where necessary.**
(a) Look Maria the British flag is red white and blue.
(b) She can't act sing or dance. She'll never get into films or on television.
(c) Well I can drive a car speak three languages play the piano and repair almost anything mechanical.
(d) She lives at flat 12 Stewart Court Oak Street Westminster London.
(e) She was born on 20th December 1961.
(f) 'Alex did you get the bread?'
'Yes it's in the kitchen Mum.'
'Thanks here's the money.'

	name	purpose	examples
,	comma	after subordinate phrases at the beginning of a sentence	If it rains, we'll change our plans. We'll change our plans if it rains. When I'd finished, I went home. I went home when I'd finished.
		before question-tags at the end of a sentence	You will do it, won't you? Ann was there, wasn't she?

2 **Put in commas where necessary.**
(a) After you have finished this work you can go.
(b) Wash your hands before you eat.
(c) If I have time I'll do it tomorrow.
(d) As soon as he got home he phoned his cousin.
(e) They'd help us if they were here wouldn't they?
(f) You aren't going to wear that hat are you?
(g) She'll be here at 7 won't she?

	name	purpose	examples
,	comma	to separate non-essential phrases from the main sentence	He's from Leeds, which is 10 miles away. That's the town where I was born. Jacob, who is 80, is in hospital. People who steal should be punished.

3   Put in commas where necessary.

(a)   He works for Simmonds which is a large manufacturing company.

(b)   Firms which employ fewer than 100 workers do not need to pay this tax.

(c)   His father who is a businessman has three cars.

(d)   Candidates who fail the exam may re-take it in June.

(e)   Tourists are advised to avoid countries where the disease is known to exist.

(f)   He's gone to Egypt where the climate is better for his health.

Apostrophes

	name	purpose	examples
'	apostrophe	to show where a letter or letters are missing in a word	it's (it is), I'm (I am), I'd (I would/had), they'll (they will), don't (do not), I can't (I cannot)
		sometimes for an unusual plural form	He agreed, but with lots of if's and but's. Her name has two l's. M.P's sit in the House of Commons.

1   Put in apostrophes where necessary.

(a)   Its raining. Youd better take a raincoat or youll get wet.

(b)   Scientists dont understand how the plane lost one of its wings.

(c)   Its fascinating to watch a bird care for its young.

(d)   Remember that this word is spelt with two cs and two ms.

	name	purpose	examples
'	apostrophe	to show possession especially for people	singular: the boy's mother, a child's toy, Mr Jones's son, a man's work
			plural: the boys' mother, children's toys, the Joneses' house, a men's club

2   Put in apostrophes where necessary.

(a)   Is that Johns car?

(b)   My fathers garden is always in good condition.

(c)   My parents home is small. They only have one bedroom.

(d)   The boys changing-room is on that side of the sports-hall. This is the girls changing-room.

(e)   Look at that girls hair.

(f)   These are the mens toilets. Those are the womens.

Inverted commas

	name	purpose	examples
' (used either singly or in pairs)	inverted commas	to mark the beginning and end of direct speech (note use of commas and capitals)	'My sister's ill,' he said. He said, 'My sister's ill.' 'How are you?' she said. 'Oh, no!' she cried. 'It's late,' he said, 'so you must go.' 'It's late,' he said. 'You must go.'

Put in inverted commas, full stops, commas, question marks, exclamation marks and capital letters where necessary. (Direct speech is underlined.)

(a) you look tired she said
(b) he said you should get a car
(c) your friend phoned she said and i told him you were out
(d) the children are asleep mary said they had a hard day
(e) move and i'll shoot he warned
(f) what time is he coming she asked he'll be hungry
(g) i'd like to live in england said max if the weather were better

	name	purpose	examples
' (used either singly or in pairs)	inverted commas	to emphasise a word or to indicate a foreign word or unusual use of a word	Don't begin a sentence with 'but'. The 'shinkansen' is a Japanese train. Radar is the 'eyes' of the defence system.
		sometimes round titles of books, films etc.	Have you read 'Treasure Island'? Shakespeare wrote 'Hamlet'. I saw a film called 'Young Love'.

Put in inverted commas where necessary.

(a) At American universities, first-year students are freshmen and second-year students are sophomores.
(b) We're studying Othello at school.
(c) The brain of the machine is this computer here.
(d) If you want a marriage partner in Japan, you go to an omiai.
(e) I've seen Gone with the Wind three times.

Spelling: noun plurals

1

	Singular	Plural	Points
final -s, -ss, -ch, -sh, -x	bus, boss, church, brush, box	buses, bosses, churches, brushes, boxes	add -es
final -y	boy, donkey, tray, valley	boys, donkeys trays, valleys	add -s if final -y follows vowel (a,e,i,o,u)
	fly, lady, body, lorry	flies, ladies, bodies, lorries	drop -y and add -ies if -y follows consonant
	sheep, fish	sheep, fish	no change in plural

Put the words in brackets into the correct plural forms.

(a) We send you our best (wish) and many (kiss).
(b) He bought a dozen (box) of (match).
(c) For Christmas he gave his sons (watch) and his daughters (dress).
(d) The (boy) are doing very well in their (study).
(e) She collects children's (toy) from different (country).
(f) (Library) are usually closed on (Sunday).
(g) (Family) of (monkey) have different (way) of looking after their (baby).
(h) He has 30 cows, 65 pigs and over 80 (sheep).
(i) i often go to the river to see the birds and the (fish).

	Singular	Plural	Points
final *-f, -fe,*	knife, shelf, self, life, wife	knives, shelves, selves, lives, wives	many nouns drop *-f, -fe* and add *-ves*
	roof, safe, handkerchief	roofs, safes, handkerchiefs	the others just add *-s*
final *-o*	tomato, potato, volcano, hero	tomatoes, potatoes, volcanoes, heroes	many nouns add *-es*
	piano, photo, kilo	pianos, photos, kilos	the others just add *-s*
irregular	child, tooth, man, woman, foot	children, teeth, men, women, feet	

Put the words in brackets into the correct plural forms.
(a)   Be careful, children. You'll hurt (yourself) with those sharp (knife).
(b)   Their (wife) waved their (handkerchief) until the train had disappeared from view.
(c)   Three people have recently lost their (life) falling from high (roof).
(d)   He bought two (kilo) of (tomato).
(e)   Here are some (photo) of famous (hero) of the Second World War.
(f)   (Woman) can damage their (foot) by not wearing suitable shoes.
(g)   (Child) should brush their (tooth) twice a day.

Spelling: verbs ending in *-y*

Verbs	3rd person singular present simple tense	Regular *-ed* form	Points
play, obey, employ, say	plays, obeys employs, says	played, obeyed, employed	*-y* after vowel *(a,e,i,o,u)* just adds *-s, -ed*
cry, study, worry, fly	cries, studies, worries, flies	cried, studied worried	drop *-y* after consonant, add *-ies, -ied*

Arrange the following verbs into two groups according to the spelling of the 3rd person singular present simple tense (some have irregular past tenses).
(a)   like *play: plays* (just add *-s*)   (b)   like *cry: cries* (drop *-y*, add *-ies*)

stay   copy   marry   display   buy
carry   destroy   occupy   multiply   dry

Put the verbs in brackets into the 3rd person singular present simple.
(c)   In the city everyone (hurry) everywhere and (try) to earn a lot of money.
       Someone in the country (enjoy) the peace and quiet of nature.
(d)   A man who (spy) against his own country (betray) his own people and, if he is caught, (pay) with his life.

Put the verbs in brackets into the -ed form (past simple or past participle).

(e) The man said the train for Leeds was (delay) until they were (satisfy) that the track was safe.

(f) I (apply) for the job, and was (annoy) when they said that I was not (qualify) for it.

Spelling: *-ing* form and regular *-ed* past tense/past participle

1

One-syllable verbs

Verbs	*-ing* form	Regular *ed* form	Points
wait, help, rain	waiting, helping, raining	waited, helped, rained	most verbs just add *-ing, -ed*
stop, stir, swim	stopping, stirring, swimming	stopped, stirred	final single consonant after **one vowel** doubles
write, care, hope, come	writing, caring, hoping, coming	cared, hoped	final single *-e* after consonant is dropped
lie, die, tie	lying, dying, tying		final *-ie* replace with *-y*
Note: *-y, -w, -x* are never doubled, e.g. staying, stayed, blowing, boxing, boxed			

Arrange the following verbs into three groups according to the spelling of the *-ing* form.
(a) like *wait: waiting* (add *-ing*)
(b) like *stop: stopping* (double final consonant, add *-ing*)
(c) like *write: writing* (drop *-e*, add *-ing*)

sleep	get	give	close	hit	read	put	bore
dig	fail	cure	trim	lose	wear	clean	win
wipe	plug	need	shut	drop	start	score	lean

Put the verbs in brackets into the *-ing* form.
(d) John's (sit) in the (live)-room, (watch) television and (eat) a sandwich. The dog is (lie) at his feet. I'm (cut) some more sandwiches.
(e) We're (have) a party on Saturday. We're (look) forward to (see) you there. We've been (plan) it for weeks. We're (die) to see you again.

Put the verbs in brackets into the regular *-ed* form.
(f) She (slow) down, (stop), (rub) her eyes and (stare) at the tall man who had (shout) and (step) out in front of her.
(g) That night she (phone) me. In a (tire) voice, she (beg) me not to leave her. 'I'm (scare). Don't go. I …' She (pause).

Two-syllable verbs ending in one consonant after one vowel

Verbs	*-ing* form	Regular *-ed* form	Points
'listen 'answer 'visit	listening answering visiting	listened answered visited	stress on *first* syllable: just add *-ing, -ed*
	Main exception: final *-l*, e.g. 'travel, travelling, travelled		
be'gin pre'fer re'gret	beginning preferring regretting	preferred regretted	stress on *second* syllable: double final consonant
	Note: *-y,-w,-x* never doubled, e.g. obeying, allowed, relaxed		

Write the verbs in brackets in the correct *-ing* form. The stress is given.
(a) Catherine's (be'gin) her new job tomorrow.
(b) Listen to that noise! What's ('happen)?
(c) He spends a lot of time ('travel) abroad.
(d) They're ('open) a new shop in Oxford next month.
(e) I apologise for (for'get) your birthday.
(f) Canada is now (per'mit) tourists to enter the country without visas.
(g) He's ('sharpen) his pencils.
(h) I like to spend my holidays (re'lax) on the beach.

Write the verbs in brackets in the correct past tense. The stress is given.
(i) My grandfather ('suffer) from very bad headaches.
(j) She said she (pre'fer) coffee to tea.
(k) The firm (al'low) the workers to go home early during the very hot weather.
(l) When they heard I was ill, they ('cancel) the meeting.
(m) He (ad'mit) to the police that he had stolen the money.
(n) I ('offer) him some money, but he wasn't interested.
(o) She (re'gret) that she couldn't come with us.
(p) Luckily no one was in the house when the explosion (oc'cur).

Spelling: miscellaneous points

1

Words	Points
also, almost, although, already, altogether, always etc.	only one *-l*
careful, useful, awful, wonderful, helpful, successful etc.	only one *-l*
taught (past of 'teach') caught (past of 'catch')	*au* not *ou*

Complete the correct spelling of the incomplete words.
(a) Al____gh it was raining, we decided to go for a walk.
(b) He has three sons and two daughters, that's five children al____er.

(c)   I'm al____s tired, doctor. I never have any energy.
(d)   She's al____y finished. Wasn't she quick?
(e)   I've known him al____t all my life.
(f)   What a won____l present! Thank you very much.
(g)   The weather was aw____l. It was cold, wet and windy.
(h)   Thank you for being so he____l when I was in trouble.
(i)   I find a typewriter very us____l in my work.
(j)   This work isn't very good. Please be more ca____l.
(k)   This year our teacher is Miss Harley. Last year Mr Weeks t____t us.
(l)   I missed the 10.15 train, but I c____t the 10.25.

2

Words	Points
whose, who's	*whose* = of whom (*Whose* pen is this?) *who's* = who is (*Who's* at the door?)
its, it's	*its* = of it (The dog ate *its* food.) *it's* = it is (*It's* hot today.)
four, fourteen, forty	note *or* in *forty*

Choose the correct item in each pair.
(a)   A woman (whose, who's) husband is dead is called a widow.
(b)   (Whose, Who's) at the door? Can you go and see, please?
(c)   I don't know (whose, who's) money this is.
(d)   I don't know (whose, who's) coming to the party.
(e)   Students (whose, who's) results are bad must take the exam again.
(f)   She's very interested in Brazil and (its, it's) history.
(g)   (Its, It's) very hot today, isn't it?
(h)   I knew it was a giraffe because of (its, it's) long neck.
(i)   The firm has decided to change (its, it's) name.
(j)   I think (its, it's) going to rain.

Spell these numbers: (k) **4** (l) **14** (m) **40** (n) **44**

3

Words	Points
necessary, accommodation, address, success, different, possible, etc.	note double consonants
copier, dirtiest, laziness, happily, beautiful etc.	final *-y* after consonant changes to *-i* before *-er, -est, -ness, -ly, -ful*
system, mystery, pyramid, etc.	note: *-y-* not *-i*

Put in the missing double letters in the incomplete words.
(a)   Is it po___ible to take a di___erent train?
(b)   Can you give me any a___re___es of student a___o___dation?
(c)   Hard work, not luck, is nece___ary for examination su___e___.

Make a suitable word from each word in brackets.

(d) He's very lazy. He's the (lazy) person I know.
(e) It's a very (beauty) part of the country.
(f) We have a very good photo-(copy) in our office.
(g) The birth of their daughter brought them a lot of (happy).
(h) I think the streets are (dirty) now than they were ten years ago.

Put the missing letter in each word in brackets.

(i) The police don't know what happened. It's a complete (m___stery).
(j) Tokyo has a very good public transport (s___stem).
(k) Have you seen the (p___ramids) of Egypt?

4

Silent letter words (silent letter in brackets)	
guard, guess etc. (u)	school, character etc. (h)
climb, comb etc. (b)	knee, knife etc. (k)
doubt, debt etc. (b)	autumn, column etc. (n)
exhibition, exhausted etc. (h)	receipt, psychological etc. (p)
hour, honest etc. (h)	write, wrong etc. (w)

Put in the missing silent letters in each incomplete word.

(a) Did you com_ your hair before you went to sc_ool this morning?
(b) Of course we were ex_austed after clim_ing the mountain.
(c) That's our first g_est _nocking at the door.
(d) I think autum_ is the _rong time to go there. Summer is better.
(e) We need an _onest man with a good c_aracter.
(f) The assistant forgot to give me a recei_t when I bought the g_itar.
(g) There is no dou_t that it is the best ex_ibition for years.
(h) She cut her _nee with a _nife.
(i) It took me an _our to _rite the letter.

Uncountable Nouns

We call some nouns 'uncountable' because they are normally singular only and we cannot count them. We do not use 'a(n)' or a plural verb with these nouns.

e.g.   work   progress   weather   money   transport
        rice   furniture   advice   paper   knowledge
        hair   luggage   bread   water   information

Note 1:
We can make some of these words countable by using the word 'piece'.

    He gave me a piece of advice.
    She had three pieces of luggage.

Note 2:
We can sometimes use uncountable nouns as ordinary, countable nouns if the meaning is different from the general use.

    Two teas, please. (teas = cups of tea)
    'The Works of Shakespeare' (works = plays, poems)
    She was reading a paper. (paper = newspaper)
    There's a hair in my soup. (hair = one single hair)

The British Isles

The British Isles are the islands off the north-west of the continent of Europe. Britain (or Great Britain) consists of England, Scotland and Wales. The United Kingdom consists of Britain and Northern Ireland. The Republic of Ireland is a separate, independent country. Match each country, city and sea below (in capital letters) with the correct number on the map.

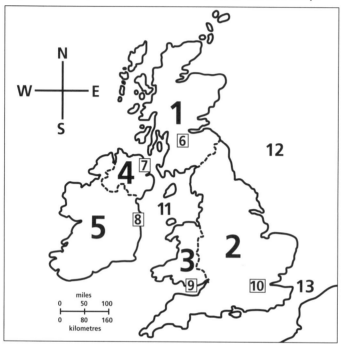

ENGLAND (population 46 million) is the largest country in the British Isles. The capital, **LONDON** (5 million), is also the capital of Britain, the seat of government and the home of the Queen.

SCOTLAND (5 million) is in the north of Britain. The language is English but 1.5% of Scots also speak Gaelic. **EDINBURGH** (0.4 million) is the capital. The Edinburgh Festival of Music and the Arts is held every year.

WALES (3 million) is in the west of Britain. English is the main language, but 25% of the people also speak Welsh and 1% speak only Welsh. The capital is **CARDIFF** (0.3 million) in the south of Wales.

NORTHERN IRELAND (1.5 million), also known as 'Ulster', is part of the United Kingdom. It has a large Roman Catholic minority. The capital is **BELFAST** (0.4 million).

THE REPUBLIC OF IRELAND (3 million) is also known as 'Eire'. The main language is English but Irish (Erse) is also spoken. 94% of the people are Roman Catholic. **DUBLIN** (0.6 million) is the capital.

THE NORTH SEA, east of Britain, provides fish and also valuable oil and gas from under the sea bed.

THE CHANNEL, between England and France, is only 34 kilometres wide at its narrowest. To cross to France you can go by ship or by train through the new Channel Tunnel.

THE IRISH SEA lies between Britain and Ireland.

Word Games

1 Rearrange the nonsense compound nouns in each group below so that they make nine real compound nouns.

(a)

A R M	W A R
F I L M	S E A T
N E W S	S I D E
W O R L D	C H A I R
C I N E M A	F R I E N D
B I R T H	P A P E R
G I R L	C A S E
B O O K	S T A R
S E A	D A Y

(b)

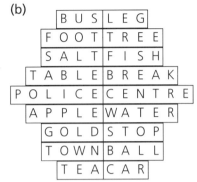

B U S	L E G
F O O T	T R E E
S A L T	F I S H
T A B L E	B R E A K
P O L I C E	C E N T R E
A P P L E	W A T E R
G O L D	S T O P
T O W N	B A L L
T E A	C A R

2 Complete the spelling of the words below using the clues to help you.

not day | | I | G | H | T |
8 | | I | G | H | T |
noun of 'see' | | I | G | H | T |
heaviness | | | I | G | H | T |
80 | | I | G | H | T | |
noun of 'high' | | | I | G | H | T |
may | | I | G | H | T |
not dark | | I | G | H | T |
not wrong | | I | G | H | T |

3 Put the missing <u>double letters</u> in the words below.

N E C E	__	A R Y
T R A V E	__	E D
F O R G O	__	E N
D I	__	E R E N T
E X C E	__	E N T
I	__	E D I A T E
B E G I	__	I N G
S U	__	__	D E D
P R E F E	__	E D

4 Make a new word from each word below by taking away **one** letter.
e.g. there – here   stand – sand

cloud	shone	coast	bright	heart	waist
stick	height	chair	talking	tries	flight
note	rain	that	skill	slow	read

5   In a word square like this one the words read the same left to right and top to bottom. Can you make your own 9 or even 16-letter square?

F	A	T
A	R	E
T	E	N

6   Fill in the puzzles by putting in the past tense of the verbs in the clues.

a)   Across   Down
    1   sing   1   sit
    3   leave   2   get
    4   take   3   lose
    6   tell   5   keep
    8   send   7   dig
    9   grow   8   see

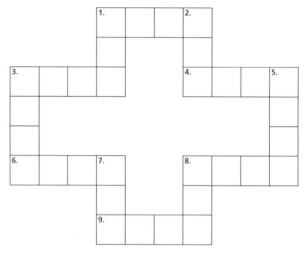

(b) Across
    3   swim
    4   come
    5   ring
    7   give
    8   think

Down
    1   catch
    2   teach
    6   find
    9   have
    10 hide

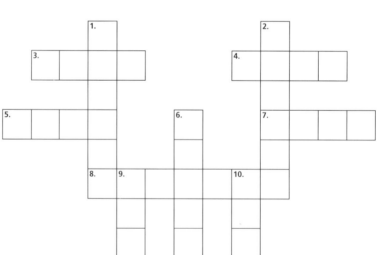

7   Make as many words as you can from BREAKFAST TIME. Each letter can be used only once in each new word. Words must be three letters or more. No proper nouns and no plurals. Then try again with UNITED NATIONS and COUNTRYSIDE.

8   For each word below give another which has a different spelling and meaning but **exactly the same pronunciation**.
e.g. past-passed   hour-our

EYE	THERE	MEET	PIECE	HOLE
WHERE	HERE	RIGHT	TWO	RED

9   Rearrange the letters of the words below to form new words according to the word on the left of each group.
e.g. birds: OPEING (Answer: pigeon)

food:	ASTOT	TAME	ASSUAGE	LOCCEATHO
	DABER	RIFUT	WINDSHAC	BEETLEGSAV
sports:	GURBY	SINENT	BLOTFALO	SHETTICAL
	XIBONG	YECKOH	SALABELB	KALTABBLES
parts of a house:	ROFO	ODOR	ROFOL	INCLIGE
	LAWL	LHAL	DIWOWN	THINECK

10   In each square below 15 words are hidden. All are in a straight line, top to bottom, left to right or going down diagonally. Can you find all the words? In the first square, three words are already done as examples.

Parts of the Body

F	I	N	G	E	R	L	L	A
A	V	O	L	F	H	A	I	R
K	H	S	A	I	A	M	P	M
E	Y	E	W	I	N	C	S	O
M	A	S	A	Z	D	R	E	Y
T	O	N	N	D	L	U	M	B
A	L	U	S	T	O	E	X	A
F	O	O	T	B	O	S	G	C
E	B	T	S	H	N	E	C	K

Animals

Z	I	C	K	I	E	C	O	W
R	E	O	A	N	D	S	W	O
A	I	R	O	T	F	O	X	L
B	E	A	R	E	V	O	G	F
S	G	I	R	A	F	F	E	N
C	H	O	R	S	E	P	L	G
E	W	E	T	H	L	I	I	O
T	I	G	E	R	I	G	O	A
H	E	L	E	P	H	A	N	T

Clothes

A	E	J	D	R	E	S	S	U
S	W	E	A	T	E	R	S	N
B	S	A	S	C	I	S	H	D
L	K	N	O	O	K	E	O	E
O	I	S	L	A	C	E	R	R
U	R	O	U	H	O	K	T	W
S	T	R	O	I	A	W	S	E
E	S	H	I	R	T	T	E	A
T	R	O	U	S	E	R	S	R

Slang

Slang is more informal than colloquial language. A lot of slang words are understood by everyone, but some slang is only used by young people or in certain regions. Here are some slang words.

nosh (food)	boo-boo (mistake)
zilch (nothing)	copper (policeman)
spud (potato)	fab (fabulous, wonderful)
nerd (fool)	sarnie (sandwich)
legless (drunk)	gobsmacked (very surprised)

Key

Dictionary Practice

Finding Words (p.1)

bank, bath, bicycle, biscuit, blood, book, both, boy, break, burn

Finding Pronunciation (p.1)

1 /ɒ/ wrong, donkey, shop, across, gone, bomb /ʌ/ company, nothing, monkey, among, love, mother, done, son, Monday **2** honest, honour, hour, exhausted, exhibition **3** sew, so / steel, steal / fair, fare / here, hear / too, two / mail, male / wait, weight / bear, bare

Finding Stress (p.1)

be'gin, 'open, 'offer, pre'fer, 'photograph, pho'tographer, photo'graphic, im'portant, 'breakfast, a'ppointment

Finding Spelling (p.1)

1 hoping, stopping, lying, hitting, picnicking, travelling, writing, beginning, putting, dying **2** radios, potatoes, heroes, kilos, studios, echoes, pianos, photos, cargoes, videos / liar, owner, beginner, bachelor, beggar, author, prisoner, burglar, translator, inspector **3** holiday, always, system, address, separate, grateful, professor, immediately, accommodation, responsible

Finding Meaning (p.2)

parts of a book: index, contents, cover, page, chapter / parts of the body: chest, thigh, thumb, ankle, wrist

clothing parts: lapel, belt, lining, zip, cuff / human sounds: sniff, cough, yawn, sneeze, hiccup / things in our pockets: wallet, comb, ticket, key, purse

Finding Different Word Parts (p.2)

1 (a) taught (b) fought (c) threw (d) froze (e) drank (f) preferred **2** nightmare, night-time, nightfall, nightcap

Topics

The Family (p.3)

1 (a) husband, wife (b) children (c) daughter, son (d) brother, sister (e) parents (f) cousins (g) uncle, aunt (h) niece, nephew **2** (a) grandchildren (b) grandparents (c) grandson, grandfather (d) grandmother, granddaughter (e) daughter-in-law (f) father-in-law, mother-in-law (g) sister-in-law (h) brother-in-law, son-in-law **3** (a) sister and brother (b) father and daughter (c) mother and son (d) cousins (e) aunt and niece (f) uncle and nephew (g) father-in-law and son-in-law (h) husband and wife (i) brothers-in-law (j) grandmother and grandson (k) grandfather and granddaughter (l) mother-in-law and daughter-in-law

Transport (p.4)

1 (a) ship (b) helicopter (c) lorry (d) (aero)plane (e) train (f) boat (g) car (h) bike (bicycle) (i) bus (j) underground train (k) van (l) motor-bike (motor-cycle) **2** (a) go (b) take (c) wait (d) arrives (e) get (f) pay (g) reaches (h) get (i) takes **3** (a) to, by, on (b) for, at (c) at, on (d) -, off

Parts of the Body (p.5)

1 (a) fingers (b) hair (c) head (d) hand (e) thumb (f) arm (g) chest (h) knee (i) sole (j) foot (k) toes (l) heel (m) leg (n) bottom (o) waist (p) back (q) elbow (r) eye (s) nose (t) mouth (u) tongue (v) ear (w) lips (x) neck (y) shoulder (z) tooth **2** (a) fingers (b) tongue (c) mouth (d) hair (e) nose (f) teeth

Clothes (p.6)

1 (a) shirt (b) tie (c) suit (d) shoes (e) cap (f) casual jacket (g) jeans (h) tee-shirt (i) underwear (j) belt (k) shorts (l) boots (m) blouse (n) skirt (o) socks (p) jacket (q) dress (r) hat (s) sweater (t) trousers (u) overcoat **2** (a) in (b) on (c) with (d) in (e) on (f) with

The Bedroom and Bathroom (p.7)

1 (a) pyjamas (b) wardrobe (c) nightdress (d) wash-basin (e) mirror (f) toilet (g) tiles (h) hanger (i) stool (j) chest of drawers (k) blanket (l) dressing-gown (m) bed (n) sheets (o) pillow (p) bath **2** (a) wardrobe (b) chest of drawers (c) pillow (d) wash-basin (e) sheets, blanket (f) dressing-gown **3** (a) on (b) on, in (c) to (d) on (e) on (f) in

The Living Room (p.8)

1 (a) light (b) ceiling (c) bookcase (d) switch (e) lamp (f) television (g) radio (h) fan (i) sofa (j) cushion (k) mat (l) armchair (m) rug (n) floor (o) carpet (p) waste-paper bin **2** (a) television, sofa, armchair (b) radio (c) fan (d) bookcase (e) waste-paper bin (f) cushion **3** (a) on (b) in (c) to (d) in (e) on (f) in

In the Street (p.9)

1 (a) signs (b) post-box (c) bus-stop (d) poster (e) lamp-post (f) queue (g) road (h) traffic-lights (i) crossroads (j) car park (k) railings (l) litter-bin (m) pedestrians (n) pavement (o) kerb (p) parking warden (q) crossing (r) parking meter (s) gutter **2** (a) queue, bus-stop (b) traffic-lights (c) crossing (d) poster (e) litter-bin (f) parking warden, parking meter **3** (a) in, at (b) in, at (c) in (d) to (e) on

The Seaside (p.10)

1 (a) hotel (b) cliff (c) rocks (d) wave (e) pier (f) horizon (g) sailing boat (h) motor-boat (i) sea (j) canoe (k) sunshade (l) swimming costume (m) towel (n) stones (o) kayak (p) rowing boat (q) tent (r) beach (s) bungalow (t) sand

The Country (p.11)

(a) waterfall (b) farm (c) spade (d) bridge (e) stream (f) barn (g) hill (h) field (i) wood (j) pond (k) forest (l) duck and duckling (m) sheep and lamb (n) cow and calf (o) valley (p) horse and foal (q) tractor (r) chicken and chick

The House (p.12)

(a) satellite dish (b) aerial (c) chimney (d) roof (e) curtain (f) shutter (g) garage (h) blind (i) stairs (j) door (k) floor (l) garden (m) gate (n) path (o) fence (p) wall

The Weather (p.13)

1 (a) sun (b) cloud (c) wind (d) rain (e) fog (f) mist (g) snow (h) forecast **2** (a) changeable (b) wet (c) dry (d) clear (e) cloudy (f) hot (g) warm (h) mild (i) cold (j) freezing **3** (a) 2 (b) 4 (c) 6 (d) 3 (e) 1 (f) 5

Going Shopping (p.14)

1 (a) assistant (b) manager (c) customers (d) shelves (e) cashier (f) basket (g) queue (h) check-out (i) trolley (j) till **2** (a) spend (b) need (c) buy (d) sell (e) push (f) look for (g) find (h) take (i) pay (j) complain **3** (a) round (b) for (c) at (d) in front of (e) on (f) for (g) from (h) in (i) in (j) to **4** (a) box (b) bottle (c) tin (d) carton (e) jar (f) tube (g) packet (h) bottle (i) box (j) bottle, tube (k) carton, tin, bottle (l) jar, tube (m) jar (n) tin (o) jar (p) packet (q) packet (r) tin, tube (s) packet **5** (a) 3 (b) 7 (c) 4 (d) 1 (e) 6 (f) 5 (g) 2

Work (p.16)

1 (a) 7 (b) 5 (c) 6 (d) 1 (e) 2 (f) 3 (g) 4 **2** (a) interview (b) experience (c) qualifications (d) skills (e) personal qualities (f) wages (g) hours **3** (a) 3 (b) 5 (c) 6 (d) 2 (e) 7 (f) 1 (g) 4 **4** (a) footballer (b) farmer (c) actress (d) librarian (e) labourer (f) secretary (g) lawyer (h) porter (i) mechanic (j) journalist (k) businessman (l) priest (m) carpenter (n) waiter (o) scientist

Education (p.18)

1 (a) play-school (b) learn (c) start (d) compulsory (e) primary school (f) terms (g) pupils (h) mixed (i) staff **2** (a) secondary school (b) state school (c) private school (d) subjects (e) specialise (f) take (g) pass (h) marks (i) fail **3** (a) student (b) grant (c) fees (d) keen (e) studies (f) courses (g) last (h) graduate (i) degree **4** (a) graduate (b) teacher training college (c) classes (d) lessons (e) homework (f) mark (g) prepare (h) behave (i) strict **5** (a) at (b) at (c) in (d) on (e) to (f) with (g) at (h) from (i) to, in (j) of (k) of (l) in (m) between (n) with

Money (p.20)

1 (a) earn (b) spend (c) borrow (d) lend (e) open (f) save (g) pay (h) afford (i) pay back (j) owe **2** (a) well-off (b) hard-up (c) make ends meet (d) broke (e) in debt **3** (a) from (b) on (c) on (d) in **4** (a) 3 (b) 4 (c) 7 (d) 1 (e) 10 (f) 8 (g) 5 (h) 9 (i) 2 (j) 6. Income: b, c, f, g, h; Expenditure: a, d, e, i, j.

A Life (p.21)

1 (a) was born (b) come from (c) grow up (d) bring up (e) educate (f) move (g) join (h) leave (i) become (j) settle down **2** (a) in (b) in (c) from (d) in (e) in (f) at (g) in (h) as **3** (a) 4 (b) 5 (c) 1 (d) 6 (e) 2 (f) 3

Sport (p.23)

1 (a) 3 (b) 1 (c) 7 (d) 5 (e) 9 (f) 8 (g) 4 (h) 6 (i) 2 **2** (a) play (b) train (c) win (d) lose (e) draw (f) beat (g) score **3** (a) two nil (b) four all (c) nil all (d) thirty love (e) fifteen all (f) love fifteen **4** (a) shooting (b) table-tennis (c) basketball (d) skating (e) football (f) motor-racing (g) running (h) baseball (i) cricket (j) rugby (k) boxing (l) volley-ball (m) cycling (n) golf (o) fishing (p) tennis (q) horse-riding (r) badminton (s) skiing (t) swimming (u) hockey **5** (1) k (2) g (3) f (4) a (5) s (6) r (7) c (8) g (9) q (10) s (11) i (12) f (13) h (14) h (15) d (16) a (17) e (18) u (19) o (20) p (21) e (22) h (23) c/e/l/p (24) t (25) r (26) n (27) j (28) c (29) k (30) m

Free Time and Holidays (p.25)

1 (a) parties (b) sociable (c) dancing (d) meeting people (e) clubs (f) discos (g) go by plane (h) hotel (i) have a good time (j) sunbathe **2** (a) cultural things (b) serious (c) classical music (d) reading (e) concerts (f) libraries (g) hitch-hike (h) youth hostels (i) learn about other countries (j) visit historical places **3** (a) the open air (b) active (c) sport (d) nature (e) sporting events (f) the countryside (g) take a train (h) camp sites (i) be close to nature (j) go for walks **4** (a) to (b) at (c) on (d) on (e) at (f) to (g) at (h) about (i) of (j) at (k) to (l) by

Illness and the Doctor (p.27)

1 (a) brain (b) lungs (c) heart (d) stomach (e) doctor (f) patient (g) nurse (h) receptionist (i) chemist **2** (a) examine (b) treat (c) suffer (d) cure (e) operate (f) look after (g) keep (h) ache **3** (a) in (b) to (c) for (d) to (e) to (f) with (g) on **4** (a) 4 (b) 3 (c) 6 (d) 1 (e) 7 (f) 2 (g) 8 (h) 5

In the Morning (p.29)

1 (a) shower (b) comb (c) briefcase (d) soap (e) hairbrush (f) newspaper (g) electric razor (h) alarm clock (i) toothbrush (j) teeth (k) clothes (l) pyjamas **2** d, f, h, b, j, c, a, r, k, e, q, g, n, i, o, p, l, m **3** (a) wear (b) put on (c) dress (d) put on (e) wear (f) dress

The Telephone (p.31)

1 (a) 2 (b) 3 (c) 5 (d) 1 (e) 4 **2** (a) 4 (b) 6 (c) 5 (d) 8 (e) 9 (f) 1 (g) 7 (h) 2 (i) 3 (j) 11 (k) 10 **3** (a) wrong number (b) engaged (c) long-distance (d) rates (e) operator (f) off-peak (g) interference (h) directory (i) directory enquiries (j) call-box (k) receiver

Watching Television (p.32)

1 (a) 5 (b) 3 (c) 6 (d) 9 (e) 4 (f) 2 (g) 7 (h) 1 (i) 8 **3** (a) turn off (b) record (c) turn on (d) switch (e) plan (f) look up

How To Do Things

How to do the Washing Up (p.33)

1 (a) washing-up liquid (b) tap (c) sink (d) draining-board (e) cupboard (f) drawer (g) cloth (h) sponge (i) brush (j) dishes **2** (2) turn on, fill, turn off (3) add (5) rinse (6) drain (7) dry (8) put away

How to make an English Breakfast (p.34)

1 (a) toaster) (b) napkin (c) frying-pan (d) teapot (e) bowl (f) salt (g) jug (h) tea-bag (i) glass (j) table-cloth (k) pepper (l) kettle **2** (1) lay (2) boil (3) pour (4) add, stir (5) spread (6) fry (8) clear away

How to do Keep-Fit Exercises (p.35)

1 (1) stand, hang (2) raise (3) turn, move (4) lower **2** (2) hold (3) lean (4) bend, bring, touch (5) straighten

How to use a Radio/Cassette Player (p.36)

1 (a) knob (b) batteries (c) controls (d) buttons (e) point (f) lead (g) plug (h) switch **2** (1) plug in (2) switch on (3) press (4) turn down, turn (5) turn up (8) switch off (9) unplug

Related Word Groups

Basic Adjectives (p.37)

1 (a) 5 (b) 3 (c) 2 (d) 4 (e) 1 **2** (a) 3 (b) 1 (c) 4 (d) 5 (e) 2 **3** (a) 4 (b) 5 (c) 2 (d) 1 (e) 3 **4** (a) 5 (b) 4 (c) 2 (d) 3 (e) 1 **5** (a) 3 (b) 5 (c) 1 (d) 2 (e) 4 **6** (a) 2 (b) 1 (c) 4 (d) 5 (e) 3

Basic Adjectives: opposites (p.38)

1 (a) good (b) fat (c) thick (d) late (e) deep (f) hot **2** (a) heavy (b) dark (c) young (d) casual (e) major (f) new **3** (a) small (b) wide (c) busy (d) wealthy (e) smooth (f) calm **4** (a) blunt (b) safe (c) public (d) wonderful (e) clean (f) short **5** (a) empty (b) guilty (c) easy (d) huge (e) tight (f) low **6** (a) slow (b) nice (c) cheap (d) wrong (e) weak (f) dry **7** (a) stupid (b) sad (c) rude (d) soft (e) ugly (f) quiet

Verbs (p.40)

1 (a) 4 (b) 1 (c) 5 (d) 3 (e) 2 **2** (a) 4 (b) 3 (c) 5 (d) 1 (e) 2 **3** (a) 3 (b) 5 (c) 2 (d) 1 (e) 4 **4** (a) 2 (b) 1 (c) 4 (d) 5 (e) 3 **5** (a) 3 (b) 5 (c) 4 (d) 1 (e) 2

Action Verbs (p.41)

1 (a) driver (b) cleaner (c) artist (d) hairdresser (e) athlete (f) dressmaker (g) hairdresser (h) cleaner (i) athlete (j) dressmaker (k) artist (l) driver **2** (a) dentist (b) soldier (c) pilot (d) gardener (e) postman (f) teacher (g) teacher (h) postman (i) solider (j) gardener (k) pilot (l) dentist

Adjectives Describing Character (p.42)

1 (a) sociable (b) adventurous (c) impatient **2** (a) easy-going (b) talkative (c) ambitious **3** (a) naughty (b) lazy (c) cheerful **4** (a) selfish (b) sensible (c) optimistic **5** (a) tidy (b) polite (c) imaginative **6** (a) polite (b) lazy (c) sensible (d) optimistic (e) sociable (f) cheerful (g) naughty (h) impatient (i) talkative (j) tidy (k) easy-going (l) ambitious (m) adventurous (n) selfish (o) imaginative

People's Appearance (p.43)

1 (a) short (b) elderly (c) bald (d) glasses (e) his arms folded (f) formally dressed (g) striped (h) well-pressed (i) well-polished shoes / (a) strongly-built (b) in his thirties (c) straight (d) bracelet (e) his hands on his hips (f) casually-dressed (g) checked (h) patched (i) trainers **2** (a) slim (b) middle-aged (c) wavy (d) necklace (e) her hands clasped (f) neatly-dressed

(g) spotted (h) smart (i) high-heeled shoes / (a) average height (b) teenage (c) curly (d) bow
(e) her hands by her sides (f) untidily-dressed (g) plain (h) baggy (i) sandals

Materials (p.45)

(a) wool (b) glass (c) paper (d) cotton (e) denim (f) stone (g) leather (h) metal (i) brick (j) plastic
(k) wood (l) iron (m) steel (n) china (o) rubber

Geographical Words (p.45)

(a) 4 (b) 8 (c) 1 (d) 5 (e) 9 (f) 2 (g) 3 (h) 11 (i) 7 (j) 12 (k) 6 (l) 10

Word Building

'-ful' and '-less' (p.46)

(a) useful (b) useless (c) painless (d) painful (e) homeless (f) helpful (g) sleepless (h) hopeful
(i) tasteless

'Interesting' and Interested' etc. (p.46)

(a) exciting (b) excited (c) relaxed (d) relaxing (e) satisfied (f) satisfying (g) boring (h) bored
(i) frightened (j) frightening (k) annoying (l) annoyed

'-er' and '-or' (p.47)

(a) worker (b) visitor (c) cleaner (d) actor (e) driver (f) employer (g) manager (h) director
(i) operator (j) maker (k) painter (l) builder (m) collector (n) sailor (o) speaker

'-ist' and '-an' (p.47)

(a) Christian (b) typist (c) politician (d) American (e) pianist (f) scientist (g) electrician (h) cyclist
(i) artist (j) guitarist (k) Roman (l) novelist

'Hourly', 'Daily' etc. (p.47)

(a) daily (b) weekly (c) yearly (d) hourly (e) fortnightly (f) monthly

'-en' (p.48)

(a) tighten (b) loosen (c) brighten (d) sharpen (e) deafen (f) widen (g) lengthen (h) strengthen

Number + Noun (p.48)

(a) five-mile (b) ten-minute (c) 200-page (d) 20-storey (e) two-week (f) ten-metre
(g) six-month (h) five-country (i) two-ton

'un-', 'dis-', 'in-', 'im-', 'il-', 'ir-' (p.49)

1 (a) unwell (b) unnecessary (c) unhealthy (d) unpleasant (e) unemployed (f) unpunctual
(g) unfair **2** (a) untidy (b) unfriendly (c) unsatisfactory (d) unusual (e) unconscious
(f) unsuccessful (g) unhurt **3** (a) unlock (b) unpack (c) untie (d) unwrap (e) undo (f) undress
4 (a) irregular (b) incorrect (c) illegal (d) inconvenient (e) impolite (f) informal (g) dishonest

Adverbs of Manner (p.50)

(a) stupidly (b) continuously (c) heroically (d) noisily (e) truthfully (f) dramatically (g) hard
(h) angrily (i) publicly (j) strangely (k) tidily (l) completely, absolutely

Compound Nouns (p.51)

1 (a) a birthday-party (b) a question-mark (c) a college library (d) a university student (e) office
furniture (f) work clothes (g) a lorry-driver (h) a television programme (i) a government
building (j) an evening class (k) a shop-window (l) a bread-knife (m) an exercise-book
(n) a ticket inspector (o) a toothbrush (p) a stamp-album (q) a road-map (r) a shoelace
(s) orange-juice (t) a book-list (u) a film magazine (v) a camera shop (w) a tourist bus
2 (a) stamp collections (b) city-centres (c) teacups (d) concert-halls (e) family doctors
(f) picture-frames (g) dog owners (h) car-wheels (i) airline pilots (j) matchboxes (k) handbags
(l) garden chairs

Word Forms (p.52)

(1) decision, decide (2) congratulate, congratulations (3) permit, permission (4) invitation, invite (5) arrival, arrive (6) depart, departure (7) complain, complaint (8) argue, argument (9) importance, important (10) difficult, difficulty (11) height, high (12) arrangement, arrange (13) bleed, blood (14) practice, practise (15) description, describe (16) explanation, explain (17) enjoy, enjoyable (18) fly, flight (19) signature, sign (20) meet, meeting (21) hot, heat (22) suit, suitable (23) relaxation, relax (24) choose, choice (25) legal, legalise (26) modernise, modern (27) industry, industrial (28) agricultural, agriculture (29) simple, simplify (30) admit, admission (31) freedom, free (32) weigh, weight (33) noisy, noise (34) safety, safe (35) dangerous, danger (36) peace, peaceful (37) lose, loss (38) mix, mixture (39) dirty, dirt (40) violent, violence (41) measurement, measure (42) kind, kindness (43) (a) happily (b) happy (c) happiness (44) (a) success (b) succeed (c) successful (45) (a) die (b) dead (c) death

Idioms

Verb Phrases (p.55)

1 (a) make your bed (b) make a list (c) make an appointment (d) make your breakfast (e) make sure (f) make a noise **2** (a) make a decision (b) make enquiries (c) make plans (d) make some money (e) make friends (f) make an effort **3** (a) take care (b) take a photo (c) take an exam (d) take a seat (e) take any notice (f) take place **4** (a) have a bath (b) have breakfast (c) have a game of tennis (d) have fun (e) have a party (f) have a rest **5** (a) keep fit (b) keep still (c) keep calm (d) keep a record (e) keep awake (f) keep quiet **6** (a) do my shopping (b) do the housework (c) do some work (d) do exercises (e) do me good (f) do a lot of harm **7** (a) get married (b) get a lot of money (c) get flu (d) get a train (e) get ready

'Touch' (p.57)

(a) keep in touch (b) get out of touch (c) get in touch

Prepositional Phrases (p.57)

1 (a) at home (b) at work (c) at the sea side (d) at school (e) at first (f) at least (g) at once (h) at last **2** (a) on time (b) on fire (c) on foot (d) on holiday (e) on business (f) on the one hand (g) on the other hand (h) on second thoughts **3** (a) in person (b) in time (c) in prison (d) in a mess (e) in trouble (f) in love (g) in tears (h) in a hurry **4** (a) by mistake (b) by post (c) by phone (d) by chance (e) by car (f) by bus (g) by all means (h) by the way **5** (a) out of date (b) out of doors (c) out of order (d) out of control (e) out of breath (f) out of work

Pairs (p.59)

1 (a) more or less (b) so and so (c) on and off (d) yes and no **2** (a) likes and dislikes (b) little by little (c) do's and don'ts (d) peace and quiet

Time (p.59)

(a) ages (b) the other day (c) so far (d) from now on (e) one day (f) for good

'Mind' (p.59)

(a) on your mind (b) change your mind (c) make up your mind (d) mind your head (e) I don't mind (f) read your mind

Things We Say (p.60)

1 (a) 4 (b) 3 (c) 2 (d) 1 **2** (a) 4 (b) 1 (c) 2 (d) 3 **3** (a) 4 (b) 3 (c) 2 (d) 1 **4** (a) 2 (b) 3 (c) 1 (d) 4

Miscellaneous

Abbreviations (p.61)

1 (a) a.m. (b) p.m. (c) etc. (d) e.g. (e) PS (f) US (g) c/o (h) Rd (i) PTO **2** (a) ft (b) ins (c) lbs
(d) BC (e) AD (f) i.e. (g) EU (h) UK

Reading Dates and Numbers (p.62)

1 (a) … 6th April (or: April 6) 1743 (b) … £2.35 (c) … 370 4492 (d) … 1276
(e) 1cm = 0.3937 ins **2** (a) … the fourth of May nineteen thirty-seven (b) … four pounds
fifty each (c) four oh eight nine double-one seven (d) … twelve thousand seven hundred
and fifty pounds (e) one pound is (or: equals) nought point four five four kilograms

Punctuation Marks (p.63)

(a) inverted commas (b) exclamation mark (c) full stop (d) question mark (e) capital letter
(f) small letter (g) apostrophe (h) hyphen (i) comma (j) brackets

Punctuation

Full stops, question marks, exclamation marks (p.63)

(a)   We've received a letter from Mr A. W. Holden. Have you seen it?
(b)   He arrives on 17 Sept. on BA flight 301. He'll stay in U.K. till the following Thurs.
        before going to the U.S.A., Japan and Australia. What a journey! Will Sue meet him
        at the airport?
(c)   Go! Get out! Now! It's dangerous! Can't you see?
(d)   She asked me if the U.S. is in the E.U. What a question!
(e)   What are you doing? Are you going out? Remember to take your key.

Commas (p.64)

1
(a)   Look, Maria, the British flag is red, white and blue.
(b)   She can't act, sing or dance. She'll never get into films or on television.
(c)   Well, I can drive a car, speak three languages, play the piano and repair almost
        anything mechanical.
(d)   She lives at Flat 12, Stewart Court, Oak Street, Westminster, London.
(e)   She was born on 20th December, 1961.
(f)   'Alex, did you get the bread?'
        'Yes, it's in the kitchen, Mum.'
        'Thanks, here's the money.'

2
(a)   After you have finished this work, you can go.
(b)   Wash your hands before you eat.
(c)   If I have time, I'll do it tomorrow.
(d)   As soon as he got home, he phoned his cousin.
(e)   They'd help us if they were here, wouldn't they?
(f)   You aren't going to wear that hat, are you?
(g)   She'll be here at 7, won't she?

3
(a)   He works for Simmonds, which is a large manufacturing company.
(b)   Firms which employ fewer than 100 workers do not need to pay this tax.
(c)   His father, who is a businessman, has three cars.
(d)   Candidates who fail the exam may re-take it in June.
(e)   Tourists are advised to avoid countries where the disease is known to exist.
(f)   He's gone to Egypt, where the climate is better for his health.

Apostrophes (p.65)

1

(a) It's raining. You'd better take a raincoat or you'll get wet.

(b) Scientists don't understand how the plane lost one of its wings.

(c) It's fascinating to watch a bird care for its young.

(d) Remember that this word is spelt with two c's and two m's.

2

(a) Is that John's car?

(b) My father's garden is always in good condition.

(c) My parents' home is small. They only have one bedroom.

(d) The boys' changing-room is on that side of the sports-hall. This is the girls' changing-room.

(e) Look at that girl's hair.

(f) These are the men's toilets. Those are the women's.

Inverted commas (p.65)

1

(a) 'You look tired,' she said.

(b) He said, 'You should get a car.'

(c) 'Your friend phoned,' she said, 'and I told him you were out.'

(d) 'The children are asleep,' Mary said. 'They had a hard day.'

(e) 'Move and I'll shoot!' he warned.

(f) 'What time is he coming?' she asked. 'He'll be hungry.'

(g) 'I'd like to live in England,' said Max, 'if the weather were better.'

2

(a) At American universities, first-year students are 'freshmen' and second-year students are 'sophomores'.

(b) We're studying 'Othello' at school.

(c) The 'brain' of the machine is this computer here.

(d) If you want a marriage partner in Japan, you go to an 'omiai'.

(e) I've seen 'Gone with the Wind' three times.

Spelling: noun plurals (p.66)

1 (a) wishes, kisses (b) boxes, matches (c) watches, dresses (d) boys, studies (e) toys, countries (f) libraries, Sundays (g) families, monkeys, ways, babies (h) sheep (i) fish **2** (a) yourselves, knives (b) wives, handkerchiefs (c) lives, roofs (d) kilos, tomatoes (e) photos, heroes (f) women, feet (g) children, teeth

Spelling: verbs ending in '-y' (p.67)

(a) stay, destroy, display, buy (b) carry, copy, marry, occupy, multiply, dry (c) hurries, tries, enjoys (d) spies, betrays, pays (e) delayed, satisfied (f) applied, annoyed, qualified

Spelling: '-ing' form and regular '-ed' past tense/past participle (p.68)

1 (a) sleep, fail, need, read, wear, start, clean, lean (b) dig, get, plug, trim, shut, hit, drop, put, win (c) wipe, give, cure, close, lose, score, bore (d) sitting, living, watching, eating, lying, cutting (e) having, looking, seeing, planning, dying (f) slowed, stopped, rubbed, stared, shouted, stepped (g) phoned, tired, begged, scared, paused **2** (a) beginning (b) happening (c) travelling (d) opening (e) forgetting (f) permitting (g) sharpening (h) relaxing (i) suffered (j) preferred (k) allowed (l) cancelled (m) admitted (n) offered (o) regretted (p) occurred

Spelling: miscellaneous points (p.69)

1 (a) although (b) altogether (c) always (d) already (e) almost (f) wonderful (g) awful (h) helpful (i) useful (j) careful (k) taught (l) caught **2** (a) whose (b) who's (c) whose (d) who's (e) whose (f) its (g) it's (h) its (i) its (j) it's (k) four (l) fourteen (m) forty (n) forty-four

3 (a) possible, different (b) addresses, accommodation (c) necessary, success (d) laziest (e) beautiful (f) copier (g) happiness (h) dirtier (i) mystery (j) system (k) pyramids **4** (a) comb, school (b) exhausted, climbing (c) guest, knocking (d) autumn, wrong (e) honest, character (f) receipt, guitar (g) doubt, exhibition (h) knee, knife (i) hour, write

The British Isles (p.72)

1 Scotland 2 England 3 Wales 4 N.Ireland 5 The Republic of Ireland 6 Edinburgh 7 Belfast 8 Dublin 9 Cardiff 10 London 11 The Irish Sea 12 The North Sea 13 The Channel

Word Games (p.73)

1 (a) armchair, film-star, newspaper, world war, cinema seat, birthday, girlfriend, bookcase, seaside (b) bus-stop, football, salt water, table leg, police car, apple tree, goldfish, town centre, tea-break **2** night, eight, sight, weight, eighty, height, might, light, right
3 necessary, travelled, forgotten, different, excellent, immediate, beginning, succeeded, preferred **4** Different answers possible. (c)loud, s(t)ick, not(e), sho(n)e, (h)eight, ra(i)n, coa(s)t, (c)hair, (t)hat, (b)right, tal(k)ing, (s)kill, hea(r)t, t(r)ies, (s)low, wai(s)t, (f)light, re(a)d
6 (a) **Across** 1 sang 3 left 4 took 6 told 8 sent 9 grew **Down** 1 sat 2 got 3 lost 5 kept 7 dug 8 saw (b) **Across** 3 swam 4 came 5 rang 7 gave 8 thought **Down** 1 caught 2 taught 6 found 9 had 10 hid **8** I, wear, their, hear, meat, write, peace, too, whole, read
9 (food): toast, bread, meat, fruit, sausage, sandwich, chocolate, vegetables
(sports): rugby, boxing, tennis, hockey, football, baseball, athletics, basketball
(parts of a house): roof, wall, door, hall, floor, window, ceiling, kitchen
10 (Parts of the body): finger, hair, arm, lips, face, hand, nose, head, eye, mouth, foot, toe, neck, leg, back (Animals): zebra, bear, cat, dog, fox, cow, wolf, giraffe, horse, sheep, tiger, elephant, pig, lion, goat (Clothes): blouse, skirt, jeans, jacket, sweater, dress, shorts, underwear, socks, coat, shirt, suit, trousers, hat, tie